Trauma Stories:

Discovering Strength Through Our Vulnerabilities

Trauma Stories:
Discovering Strength Through Our Vulnerabilities

by Marcken Volmy

Copyright © 2023 by Marcken Volmy

Scripture quotations marked MSG are taken from *THE MESSAGE*, copyright © 1993, 2002, 2018 by Eugene H. Peterson. Used by permission of NavPress. All rights reserved. Represented by Tyndale House Publishers, Inc.

All rights reserved, including the right to reproduce this book or portions of this book in any form whatsoever, without the prior written permission of the copyright owner.

Published 2023

Manufactured in the United States of America

ISBN 979-8-9884724-1-4 (hardcover)
ISBN 979-8-9870725-8-5 (paperback)
ISBN 979-8-9870725-9-2 (Ebook)

*For my wife, Edna, and children, Makayla and Nyella.
Also for every trauma survivor who had the audacity to color outside the lines of what is considered to be normal.*

Acknowledgments

If life were a person, I would say thank you for giving me a collection of tragedies, brokenness, defining moments, and redemption. Thank you to Evoke180 for your expertise, attention to detail, and passion for bringing life to these pages. Thank you to Mirna Pierre. Thank you to every past and present client who has entrusted me with their trauma story. Thank you to the trauma therapists, practitioners, and space holders in this field who have made it their life's mission to see people obtain a sense of freedom and agency over their trauma. Thank you to my lovely wife, Edna, for encouraging me throughout this process. Thank you to Sheim Francis and the entire IV His Glory team for your ongoing support. Thank you to Eddie Archer for your continued support. Thanks to Rodney Wilkinson for being a brother and a mentor. Special thanks to my Lord and Savior Jesus Christ for using someone as broken as me as a conduit to walk with those who have been maligned, broken, abandoned, and rejected by life. Last, but not least, thank you to every trauma survivor who will read this book and resolve to take ownership of their healing.

For the privacy of my clients, pseudonyms were used to protect any identifying information. All of the stories told in this book are nonfiction and are the personal stories of myself and my past clients.

Foreword

But how can people call for help if they don't know who to trust? And how can they know who to trust if they haven't heard of the One who can be trusted?

And how can they hear if nobody tells them?

And how is anyone going to tell them unless someone is sent to do it? (Romans 10:14–17, MSG)

There is tangible freedom locked inside of a story, *but* if the storyteller isn't convinced, that freedom remains locked up.

Don't read this book just to learn about trauma; read it to become courageous in creating space for your own story. This book offers the hope that it is possible to direct the influence of your past. It will strengthen your resolve to defy the fear that makes holding your story feel so out of reach.

I've known Marcken for years, and I've been a witness to his fervent attentiveness to his own traumatic experiences. With full confidence, I can promise you a couple of things.

First, I promise, you are safe in the hands of Marcken. I've seen him boldly share his story of who he is becoming throughout his journey. These same stories are shared in the pages of this book. You will be comforted by the fact that Marcken is as caring as he is inspiring.

Second, I am confident that you will get the tools you need to begin this journey. Marcken has a skill for making the most complex issues easily understandable and actionable. Receive clarity, overcome blocking beliefs, and learn what it takes to walk out the journey.

This is the only thing I ask of you as you engage with this book: show compassion toward yourself.

Pray this with me:

"God, give me the serenity to accept the people I cannot change, the courage to change the person I can, and the wisdom to know it's me."

And with this act of compassion, I hope you will allow this book to be your defining moment and to go and own your story.

—Edvardo Archer, LMFT

Contents

Acknowledgments vii
Foreword ix
Introduction 1
Chapter 1 — Storytellers: Your Story Matters 5
Chapter 2 — Office Hours: We All Need Therapy 13
Chapter 3 — Excuse Me! Trauma Affects the Mind
and Body Differently? 21
Chapter 4 — Survival Mode: Learning to Survive
Hard Times 37
Chapter 5 — Stigmatized: The Shame Behind the
Mental Health Discussion 47
Chapter 6 — EMDR Therapy: A Deep Exhale 57
Chapter 7 — Trauma and Culture 67
Chapter 8 — Fractured Connections: The Negative
Effects of Trauma on Relationships 75
Chapter 9 — The Healing Journey: What Healing
Looks Like for Trauma Survivors 83
Chapter 10 — Broken Children: Helping to Heal the
Traumatized Kid in Every Trauma Survivor 93
Chapter 11 — Round of Applause: Taking a Moment
to Celebrate Every Trauma Survivor 103
Conclusion 111
Endnotes 113

Introduction

During my undergrad days, I had a part-time temp job that consisted mainly of filing paperwork. I was not the best at multitasking, and in my attempts to carry my cup of coffee, phone, folders, and water bottle, I always seemed, like clockwork, to drop something. Just about every time this occurred, one or two of my coworkers would kindly reach over to pick up what I had dropped. I don't know if it was my male ego or my reluctance to embrace help, but I would usually say something like, "I got it, but thanks, though." The truth of the matter was that I didn't have it that day or the days leading up to that one. I was too ashamed to admit that about something as trivial as someone making the kind gesture of simply picking up an item I had dropped. We tend to treat our mental health the same way. We carry around all of this trauma and stress in our bodies, and when we begin to fumble our priorities, those close to us may try to lend a helping hand, only to be denied by our shameful fear of accepting help. Society has groomed us to repel vulnerability and embrace the so-called *strong man* and *strong woman* syndrome.

As a therapist, one of the most heartbreaking things about my job is seeing people pretend to have a handle on their trauma when they're really struggling internally. All the while, they are refusing to accept help from those who are willing to bear the load that was too heavy for them to carry in the first place. So how in the world will they ever muster up the strength to pick it back up again? Hence why I wrote *Trauma Stories*—to take you on a deep dive into my life and the lives of my past clients and frame a more nuanced context of trauma at large. Whether you realize it or not, we all have our own *trauma story*. I hope I leave you inspired to share yours after reading this.

Maybe you're someone who lacks confidence in yourself and feels stuck where you are in life. Maybe you do not feel like you are living life to the fullest. Maybe you're afraid of pursuing your lifelong goals and dreams. Your past trauma and heartbreaks have probably left you stagnant when it comes to doing some of the things you secretly hope to accomplish, like falling in love or becoming a bit more social with coworkers and neighbors. You may find it easier not to ask for help in fear of feeling like a burden to others, let alone a therapist. Like many people, you probably struggle with depression, anxiety, and childhood trauma. Have you felt like you're merely existing and not thriving in life? Maybe your ultimate aim is peace and contentment in life. You feel stuck in your career, relationship, and overall mental health. You internalize your emotions and have contemplated ways you can take your own life at times.

Trauma Stories: Discovering Strength Through Our Vulnerabilities will help you to normalize your behaviors and emotions, which are a byproduct of past traumatic experiences. There's healing in telling your story and finding a safe space with a skilled trauma therapist to help you process the internal chaos you've been grappling with. Healing doesn't have to feel elusive. It's real and available to you.

You will learn resilience by remaining consistent with therapy and learning new coping skills. You'll start to heal from your past feelings of depression, anxiety, and trauma after engaging with an eye movement desensitization reprocessing (EMDR) therapist. Trauma therapy will help your mind and body feel a sense of safety and resolve the relational disconnect in your life. You will learn to be patient with the mental health process and your journey. As you begin to heal from your trauma wounds, you will find it safer to lean into your support system.

What would it look like if you reframed your self-sabotaging mindset and started to embrace life with more expectation and passion? According to statistical data, in 2019–2020, fifty million Americans were struggling with some type of mental illness.[1] You'll learn how to clearly identify and describe your trauma in the context of storytelling. Our stories connect us and can be used as the catalyst to start our healing journey. Vulnerability is a strength, and those who are willing to begin therapy will cultivate strength to help heal and break the intergenerational trauma that continues to cycle through their family tree. You matter, your story matters, and what you decide to do with that can help you either to heal or to remain stagnant and overwhelmed.

Marcken Volmy is a licensed clinician with a specialty in EMDR therapy. Over the years, he has experienced his share of past trauma, which he has processed in EMDR therapy. Marcken understands what it's like to be on both sides of the couch, as a client and as a therapist. The premise for writing *Trauma Stories: Discovering Strength Through Our Vulnerabilities* was birthed out of a desire to help others discover what relief from their trauma looks and feels like. As a trauma therapist, Marcken Volmy clearly understands that telling your stories alone won't heal you of your traumatic stress and attachment wounds. It will, however, remove the stigma that prevents you from connecting with a trauma therapist.

Are you ready to hope again, gain a better understanding of trauma and its effects on the brain and body, be inspired to share your story, and have your story validated? Keep reading. Alongside me, you will embark on the journey of becoming a storyteller.

Chapter 1—
Storytellers: Your Story Matters

Have you ever looked up just to see the bottom? That's what the past thirty-plus years have felt like for me. It has been a constant ebb and flow of trying to find language for all the internal chaos I've experienced. I thought no one could relate to what I was going through, only to find out my story was just as relatable as the next person's.

Victoria's mother was a drug addict who paid for her addiction by sleeping with random men for money out of her apartment. Sometimes Victoria would see more than one man engaging in sexual acts with her strung-out mother, but for the most part, there were always men coming in and out of their home. One night, one of the men entered Victoria's bedroom and sexually assaulted her. Victoria was only six years old at the time.

Unfortunately, this was not the last time Victoria experienced being sexually assaulted. She had a younger brother with special needs, and he and Victoria would go days and weeks without proper food and nutrition. They also missed a lot of school days as a result of their mother's neglect. This resulted in Victoria eventually feeling like she had no choice but to scour through the dumpsters at various restaurants and fast-food locations in her neighborhood in search of some food for herself and her little brother. As Victoria got older, she and her younger brother were taken into foster care, and her mother's parental rights were terminated.

Victoria ended up developing an eating disorder and suffered from complex posttraumatic stress disorder (PTSD). She also dissociated and blocked out any recollection of her childhood abuse from the age of six until her twenty-first birthday, when something randomly triggered her. As a teen, Victoria was very defiant to any type of authority and was in and out of toxic relationships with men who would mistreat her. As an adult, she struggled to cope with the internal raging terror of her trauma. She struggled with suicide attempts, shame, and substance abuse. When Victoria started seeing me for therapy, she made some progress in our sessions, but the more she opened up in greater detail about her traumatic past, the more I realized that she wouldn't benefit much from talk therapy. So, we started EMDR. It was a journey, but I'm happy to say that Victoria is now thriving in a profession that entails helping others who are hurting and broken as well. Victoria has gained a greater sense of safety and connection in her body and mind.

Your story matters because it connects people in different ways by utilizing vulnerability as an agent of change and healing. The reason for writing trauma stories is to shed light on the power of our stories and how we're connected by them. Many of you are not fans of how your story has played out thus far. If it were up to you, you would have much rather continued to evade any subtle reminders of whatever traumatic memories you've been carrying around all these years. What if I told you that even if you're not telling your trauma story to others, you're definitely communicating it to yourself? You relive your trauma story whenever someone or something triggers you, whenever you experience a flashback or an intrusive thought. And that's not to mention the barrage of negative thoughts and beliefs that your mind consistently beats you down with on a daily basis. Trauma resides in your nervous system, and many people have been operating with a nervous system that's on overdrive and is completely depleted of safety, connection, and hope. It's okay if you don't have the wherewithal to navigate all the different layers and nuances of trauma. Don't be too hard on yourself for not having the capacity to figure it out on your own.

Many people dismiss their stories because of their negative beliefs about themselves. A common trauma response that will often come up with trauma survivors is the minimization of their story and overall experience. You dismiss your story because you truly don't believe you matter, and if you see yourself as having very little value and worth, how can you ever see any value in your own trauma story? Your trauma story matters because you do. Contrary to the negative popular opinion that's been running laps in your mind, you have a lot of worth, dignity, and value.

I don't want to make light of some of the horrific things that people have gone through, and without the proper mental health intervention and support, it's almost impossible to muster up the courage to tell your story with a sense of resilience and confidence. Trauma has become a *buzzword* in today's culture, so let's take a bird's-eye view. What exactly is trauma and what are the various types of trauma? When identifying trauma, two things are necessary: exposure and impact. If you haven't been exposed to anything or impacted by something or someone, there's a possibility that you haven't experienced trauma, and I have yet to meet this type of person.

Trauma is basically anything that overwhelms our resources and ability to cope with something. The DSM-5 definition of a trauma event states: "The person was exposed to: death, threatened death, actual or threatened serious injury, or actual or threatened sexual violence, in the following way(s): direct exposure; witnessing the trauma; learning that a relative or close friend was exposed to a trauma or indirect exposure to aversive details of the trauma, usually in the course of professional duties (e.g., first responders, medics)."[1]

Trauma can include a broader net of overwhelming events and situations, such as war, natural disasters, and the absence of things that you should've received as a child, such as nurture, safety, parental/caregiver connection, and love. Examples of traumatic experiences can be the following: humiliation; bullying; manipulation; grief; divorce; abandonment; sexual, physical, or emotional abuse. The failure to have your emotional needs met can leave a void that is felt much later in life. Trauma survivors can experience a dysregulation of emotional states, which can lead to hyperarousal, including fear, panic, and uncontrolled anger.[2]

Trauma will also have an effect on someone's interpersonal relationships, so why in the world would someone want to share their trauma story after such experiences? Everyone's reason will be different, but the one constant is that as you are healing, it gets easier to share your story, and your story can have an impact for the betterment of everyone who is touched by it, whether that connection is direct or indirect.

Earlier I mentioned that trauma resides in your nervous system, so obviously, telling your story alone will not clear out your trauma, but it will definitely put you on the right path toward embarking on your healing journey. Many of us subscribe to the misconception that vulnerability is a weakness. We perceive vulnerability as a hindrance as opposed to a strength. This shouldn't be the case. Not telling someone, especially a therapist, that you're struggling and hurting is a great disservice to you, your family, and those who deeply care about you. Vulnerability requires a level of honesty and transparency that leaves you feeling helpless and emotionally naked, but it is such a display of quiet strength. Granted, you don't want to entrust something as precious as your trauma story to someone who doesn't appreciate the beauty of mental health or your experience. But for the most part, many people will be encouraged by what you have to offer when sharing your story, especially you!

Vulnerability helps remove the mask that shame has helped you to put on and keep on. It's hard to hold on to shame and guilt when you see vulnerability as a catalyst of change in your healing journey. You have no idea who your story will inspire and the resilience that you'll slowly start to cultivate when you're telling your story through the lens of a trauma survivor as opposed to a trauma victim. What's cool about owning your story, going to therapy, and leaning into the power of vulnerability is that you and a collective of other healthy people and tools are all helping to re-author your story. It's a story that's still a work in progress along with its author, who's still slowly piecing together all the broken parts that were formed as a result of their story. These are the parts that will add color, grammar, and passion to your story. We'll also get into parts a bit more when discussing dissociation in chapter 4 and how these different parts of ourselves were formed as a result of our trauma in order to help protect and manage our internal chaos.

I wish I could say that after telling your story, you can do three or four things and you'll never have to worry about your trauma again, but why would I try to sell you the "hustle" when you've already been gracious enough to purchase this book? But I digress! Real change is slow, consistent, and intentional. We'll discuss later on, in chapter 9, how neuroplasticity, which is the brain's way of forming newer and stronger healing connections, takes place in the brain when repetition is utilized. Healing is not linear. Your story will be, and should be, different from the next person's, and that's nothing to be ashamed of. Trauma affects us all differently, so it would be naive of you to think that the pacing and progress of your story should look like someone else's. If your story is different and unique, expect the same with your transformation process. The intentionality of telling your trauma story, leaning into your support system, and engaging with a skilled trauma therapist are just some of the consistent measures that will be beneficial for you when healing from trauma.

When I say "heal," please don't think along the lines of someone "fixing" you. Healing is a continuous and ongoing process. As you take steps toward healing, you'll have these defining moments where you'll look back and reflect on the progress you've made thus far. Your mental health progress can't be measured in real time, but when you look back, you'll be able to measure if you're taking progressive steps forward or regressing backward. As you heal, you'll begin to view your trauma story with eyes of relief, gratitude, and mental clarity.

My parents, my two older siblings, and I migrated to the United States from the Bahamas by way of Haiti in the spring of 1985. I was four years old at the time. It was definitely a learning experience and cultural adjustment for us all. Before we found our own place, we moved in with relatives for about six months. Back then, minimum wage was $2.75 per hour. My mother worked a full-time housekeeping job, and my father was employed as a dishwasher at two different restaurants. Those were some lean years, but at the same time, food and gas were a lot more affordable back then. During those six months, there was very little adult supervision for me and my cousins. Both sets of parents worked tirelessly for long hours to help make ends meet for us all. On most days during the week, we would, like most kids, watch a lot of television, eat a lot of sweets, and run around the house until we passed out or got injured. I would love to say that those were some fun times, and they were, but that wasn't always the case.

I remember on one occasion, an older cousin of mine, who was still a kid himself, instructed me and a female cousin of mine to strip down to nothing. Mind you, I was five at the time and didn't think much of it. He prompted us to pretend we were having sex by instructing us to rub our genitals against each other as if we were in the act of being intimate. This relative, along with some of his friends, egged us on and thought that this was great entertainment and amusement. Me and my female cousin were both confused and uncomfortable with his instructions. To add insult to injury, years later, my cousin would bring this up as if it was something comical from our childhood experience.

It was years later, when I finally went to therapy and disclosed this incident to my therapist, that she clearly made the distinction that what I experienced that day as a five-year-old was a form of childhood sexual abuse. I should have been playing with action figures and Lego sets, but instead, I was learning about female anatomy and sexual positions. I lamented this experience not only for me but also for my female cousin who had also had her innocence stolen. We were only four and five years old, and now a Pandora's box of sexualized thoughts and behaviors was spreading its roots in both of our minds. Throughout my upbringing, I would go on to have a very toxic relationship with sex. I used it as a coping skill to numb myself from feelings of depression and inadequacy. Trauma therapy helped me to better understand how sex had become my way of soothing from other traumas such as rejection, depression, and abandonment.

Chapter Takeaways

Your story matters because it connects people in different ways by utilizing vulnerability as an agent of change and healing.

As we heal from our trauma, we help to re-author our life's narrative.

Vulnerability is a strength that can be utilized on your healing journey.

Despite all the vacillating experiences with my mental health, including the internal chaos, I had no idea just how much I had in common with other trauma survivors. Relatability was something I could really use right now. After mustering up the courage to book an appointment with a therapist, I walked up to her front door and read the sign: "Office hours are Monday–Friday from 9 a.m.–5 p.m." I actually thought about turning right back around and convincing myself that this was all a big mistake, since I seemed to be doing okay with my issues. But I knew that if I were to walk away from this, I would continue the toxic cycle of walking away from anything that I found challenging. It felt like an eternity went by, but truthfully it was nothing more than a five-second pause. I walked right through those doors and started my journey of finally going to therapy.

Chapter 2—
Office Hours: We All Need Therapy

In the fall of 2006, I was doing a little early Christmas shopping at the local mall. The woman ringing me up had a strong Brooklyn accent. "Are you from New York?" I asked her as she folded my items.

She replied, "Yeah."

Somehow we started talking about 9/11. She mentioned that she lost friends and a family member in the Twin Towers. With tears welling up in her eyes, she said, disheartened, "I can't! I just can't! I know it's been some years, but it's still hard!"

"I'm sorry," I replied.

I think about this woman quite often and wonder if she ever sat down with a therapist to fully process her traumatic grief.

*L*isa's parents divorced when she was seven. Lisa's mother placed a lot of significance and value in education, so it was quite normal for Lisa to seek validation through her impeccable academic achievements. Lisa always felt like her father understood her better, but she lived with her mother full time. She did quite well in school, but her mother never made her feel like her academic efforts were good enough.

By the time Lisa was in middle school, she started experimenting with marijuana, and later on with stronger drugs. She began to struggle with depression and anxiety, and by the time she was in high school, she was hanging out with older people who were into a lot of partying and drug use. During Lisa's high school years, she attended a party with some of her friends. She got high and ended up passing out at this party, and when she woke up, she saw a random guy on top of her raping her. Lisa froze helplessly and was in total shock. This incident ended up being one of many shameful experiences that Lisa would medicate with drugs and sex in the hopes of not having to think about it.

After high school, Lisa struggled with unhealthy dating relationships and drug addiction, which eventually led to stripping and sleeping with random men to support her drug use and pay bills. Lisa struggled with a lot of shame and feelings of unworthiness. By the time she started working with me, I noticed the pain in her voice when telling her story, and she seemed to be defeated by life. We tried EMDR for about three months. Although it was tough at first for Lisa, eventually, by the end of therapy, she was much happier and started envisioning some of the things she aspired to do both professionally and personally in life. Lisa is now a mother and thriving with her new family and support system.

Recognizing your need for help should be the first step in seeking therapy. Therapy can cover a vast array of topics: marital issues, addictive behaviors, anxiety, phobias, depression, unprocessed trauma, stress management, grief, eating disorders, suicidal ideations and attempts, maintenance care, etc. Therapy is not only for "major issues." If something is stressful and overwhelming, or if you just need some clarity and direction on something, it's important enough to speak to a therapist about. I've mentioned several times throughout this book how your "inner critic" can dismiss your trauma story and make you think you'd be wasting your time, and your therapist's time, if you were to bring up a particular topic to explore during one of your sessions. That is a long way from the truth, but unless you're able to get out of your own head and speak to an unbiased professional, you'll never know that.

The term *psychotherapy* dates back to 1890 and was coined from two Greek words, *psyche* and *therapeia*. *Psyche* means "spirit or mind," and *therapeia* means "treatment or healing."[1] In today's modern mental health and healthcare era, psychotherapy is defined as the remedy or alleviation of dysfunctional behaviors or emotional dysregulation, helping others to tap into their potential by psychological means as opposed to sociopolitical interventions and biomedical treatments.[1]

At the start of the twentieth century, therapy was considered to be rare and mainly a treatment for the "mad" or psychotic. Oddly enough, fast-forward to modern times and therapy is available to the broader public, including those dealing with typical challenges at work and at home. What led to this drastic change in how therapy was viewed occurred in the post–World War II era.[2] During World War II, many servicemen were coming back home from the war with severe PTSD symptoms. On the outside they looked fit for service, but mentally they were a shell of themselves. This led to massive discharges from the armed forces, and due to the small number of psychotherapists and physicians at that time, the need for therapists started to gain a lot more attention.

The focus on mental health at large can now be seen in courtroom trials with expert witnesses, modern TV shows, movies, and talk shows. Depending on the relational topic at hand, it seems that everyone wants to be informed by an expert in a particular field or cement their viewpoint by bringing in a therapist who can validate their perspective. You would think with all of the traction that therapy has made over the last one hundred years it would be further along, but unfortunately that is not the case. Some people create their own mental barriers as to why therapy isn't for them. The barriers that many people face that stop them from going to therapy may be the result of unprocessed trauma, the shame of being perceived as "crazy," or the financial cost of affording a decent therapist—not to mention learning to stay the course when searching for a therapist after the first couple of options have not panned out.

Whatever your reason for wanting to give up or not start your search for a therapist, let me give you a good counter argument. You can't afford not to! Let me preface this by saying that your friends and family members can only handle so much of what you're putting on their emotional plate. I would occasionally get asked, "What should I do with a friend or family member who continues to tell me all of their problems that I'm ill equipped to address and don't have the answers for or even know what to do with?" Even if you're a great listener, usually you truly do care about this person and are too close to the situation not to be emotionally invested. This can turn into a cyclical behavior that is toxic and exhausting. The term for this is *trauma dumping*. People who trauma dump will hardly ever take your advice, but they don't mind dumping all their problems on you.

A good therapist will be unbiased and help validate your trauma story simply by giving you their undivided attention. Some of you have yet to feel like, "Finally, for once in my life, someone has made me feel seen and heard." When was the last time someone looked you in the eye and affirmed how you felt, what you experienced, without once being distracted by their phone, television, or to-do list? What would it look like if you began to normalize therapy and mental health in your day-to-day conversations? For example, "I'm not available to hang out with you that day. That's when I'm scheduled to see my therapist." "Have you considered talking with a professional—you know, a counselor?" Whether it's a moment of crisis or prevention work, usually there's this awkward silence at first, but normalizing the conversation is a non-confrontational way of saying, "You need therapy, I need therapy, we all need therapy!" Therapy can be very beneficial in moments of crisis and prevention.

The more we normalize therapy, the more we'll lessen the stigma behind it. Whether you realize it or not, therapeutic principles are intertwined into our Western context. Many people utilize these techniques in their daily conversations by deconstructing their experiences into discrete thoughts and feelings to resolve conflicts among themselves.[3] These conflicts are typically framed as dialogues between the mind and the heart, the right brain and the left brain, or "this part of me" and "another part of me." I often hear people attempt to pathologize themselves and others, whether that's in humor or in all seriousness. "I'm so OCD!" "You're so bipolar!"[1] This can be a bit insensitive to those who are actually suffering from a mental illness. Finally, therapy is needed to help educate people on various mental health issues and diagnoses and ways to improve and heal from their overall mental struggles. Therapy helps to add structure and direction to interpersonal communication and engagement.[4] We frame healthy conversations through the lens of therapy.

It was December of 1992, a couple of days before Christmas. I remember staring at this old clock in my living room, and it read 6:30 p.m. My siblings and I started to worry. Usually our parents were home from work by now.

We got a call around 7:30 p.m. My sister picked up, and it was my father. He said that my mother and he were in a near-fatal car accident while heading home from work. He went on to say, "Your mother had her seat belt on and her head still smashed against the front windshield pretty violently." My mother was knocked unconscious, and my father fractured a couple of bones in the base of his neck. He was in a neck brace for several weeks. My father was discharged from the hospital the following day, but my mother would spend two more days in the hospital. She suffered a very bad concussion, her face was cut pretty severely, and one of her eyes was swollen shut. It was horrific and overwhelming as a twelve-year-old to contemplate the thought of almost losing both of my parents to such a freak accident. My mother followed up with a couple more visits with her doctor to remove some remaining glass fragments that were still lodged in her forehead.

The day after the accident was probably the first time I ever heard my father cry. As strange as it sounds, I actually felt comforted by the sound of that. For once in my life, he came across as feeling something. Usually, my father would present with an emotionally stoic affect and show very little emotion. This was common for most Caribbean men. For once, he was displaying a sense of emotional connection with his children, I thought.

Over the next several months, the rehab process was difficult for both of my parents, especially for my mom. She was out of work for at least six months. Years later, I had the privilege of working with kids in foster care and thought how the plight of many of these amazing children would have been mine had my parents not survived that day. It's been over thirty years, and I can still remember the look on my mother's face when she was discharged from the hospital. I would later process the pain and fear I felt that day with my therapist. It was emotional but much needed.

Chapter Takeaways

We can all benefit from therapy, and not just in moments of crisis. The more we normalize the conversation around therapy, the more we'll lessen the stigma behind it. The stigma is rooted in shame of what others will think of you.

A good therapist will validate you and your story.

Instead of speaking to a therapist, we trauma dump all of our issues on our friends and family.

Whenever I think of the woman at the mall that day who was discussing 9/11 with me, I wish there was more I could have said and done to comfort and help her. I wish I could have validated her pain, sat with her in the silent awkwardness of grief, and told her she doesn't have to always feel that way. The tears she shed that day while standing at her register spoke volumes to me about a pain that I was all too familiar with—a pain that I would gain a better understanding of and one day help others to process.

As I sat there and answered my therapist's questions, I felt very uncomfortable. She smiled observantly and looked at me as if she could see right through me. I felt both naked and clothed as she took an Olympic dive right into the deep recesses of my mind. After we moved past the formalities of confidentiality and my rights as a client, I was very impressed by how knowledgeable she was about trauma and its effects on the human body. Finally someone was putting language to all the anxiety, fear, and trauma I had experienced throughout most of my childhood. I learned that day about a broader definition of trauma and how the mind and body respond differently when impacted by it.

Chapter 3—
Excuse Me! Trauma Affects the Mind and Body Differently?

"Traumatized people chronically feel unsafe in their bodies: The past is alive in the form of gnawing interior discomfort. Their bodies are constantly bombarded by visceral warning signs, and, in an attempt to control these processes, they often become expert at ignoring their gut feelings and in numbing awareness of what is played out inside. They learn to hide from their selves." —Bessel A. van der Kolk[1]

*A*dam's father used to beat him daily, belittle him, and show preferential treatment to his other kids, whom he had with Adam's stepmom. "Having my stepmom treat me differently by giving them certain snacks, drinks, and clothing items that I did not receive hurt more than my dad's punches," stated Adam dishearteningly. Adam's birth mother was still living in another country at the time and had sent him to live with his father in America in hopes of making a better life for Adam. Adam's father let him know early on that there was no room for patience or grace for him.

What made things frustrating for Adam was that he would be beaten for mistakes that his step-siblings would make, and they would receive a verbal reprimand instead. Adam's father would at times beat his other children as well, but for some reason, he took a lot of his frustrations out on Adam, as if he faulted him for the things that went awry in his life. Adam's fear of his father manifested as gastrointestinal issues. He recalled sitting on the toilet for at least an hour every day after school at just the mere sight of his father when he got home. He repeated this process daily without realizing that it was linked to the trauma that he was still carrying in his body.

Fear paralyzed Adam in a lot of different ways. He developed severe anxiety and uncontrollable anger. When I started working with Adam, he had a very flat affect and hardly ever smiled. He reminded me of war veterans I've worked with in the past who were suffering from complex PTSD. Adam had to work through the layers of physical abuse, feeling unloved at the hands of his father, and the emotional abuse he suffered at the hands of his stepmother. A couple of weeks into our EMDR sessions, Adam eventually smiled, and when I mentioned it to him, it hit him that he hadn't smiled much in years.

Adam learned to gain a sense of safety for that little boy inside of him who was abused, overlooked, and treated as less than as a result of not having a trusted adult who was willing to advocate for him. Adam processed his trauma and now has his own family.

He no longer struggles with debilitating anxiety and uncontrollable anger outbursts. He now has congruence. What he feels internally matches his outward expression. It was very rewarding to see the transformation in Adam's life over those several months. EMDR therapy helped Adam to become unstuck, feel safe again, and learn how to connect with others.

When discussing trauma's effect on the body, we must first understand its effect on the mind. After experiencing a traumatic event, the brain will continue to respond as if the occurrence is still taking place. For example, if someone is held down, unable to take action of any kind, whether that's the result of a horrible car accident, rape, or a domestic violence situation, the brain continues to secrete stress chemicals long after the threat no longer exists.[1] The brain sends internal signals to ensure that it is working in harmony with the body. Psychological stresses, such as trauma, can interfere with these networks and mapping. Let's break down the different parts of the brain, and later on I'll explain how the inner workings of these parts respond to trauma.

The rational or logical part of the brain helps us to connect with and gain a better understanding of the world around us. The rational brain helps us to focus on how things and people function, goal setting, punctuality, and the management of our day-to-day life.[1]

The reptilian brain, or the base of the brain that is located in the brainstem—the oldest part of the brain—helps babies to sleep, cry, breathe, experience hunger, have body temperature awareness, and feel pain.[1] The limbic system sits right above the reptilian brain and controls your emotions by making you aware of things that are pleasurable and situations that are dangerous. Your brain has the unique ability to shape your sense of safety or threat based on its ability to repeatedly fire a certain circuitry. In other words, your brain will develop a sense of safety or fear based on the repeated stimuli exposure that it encounters on a daily basis. The limbic system and the reptilian brain make up the emotional part of your brain, which consists of a lot of the emotions and sensations that you feel.[2] As shown in figure 1 below, the limbic system contains a lot of different parts that contribute to the brain's rewiring after a traumatic event.

Limbic system

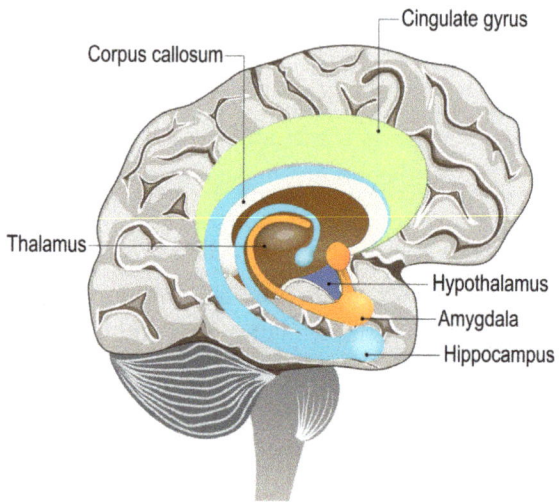

Figure 1
Limbic system, including the amygdala

The emotional part of the brain works in tandem with the central nervous system, with one major goal in mind—and that's to ensure you're safe at all times.[1] If your brain senses danger, the amygdala, which consists of two tiny almond-shaped structures that reside in the limbic system, is activated. The amygdala, which is displayed above in figure 1, remains overactive during trauma. It's like the alarm system in the brain to let us know that we're in danger. When the amygdala is activated, your adrenal glands, which are located on the top of your kidneys, release the stress hormones cortisol and adrenaline. Your airways begin to expand, your heart beats faster, and your pupils dilate. Now your body's ready to respond either in flight, fawn, fight, or freeze mode. Fawn is a trauma response that you typically experience later on, and it manifests as people-pleasing or seeking the validation of others.

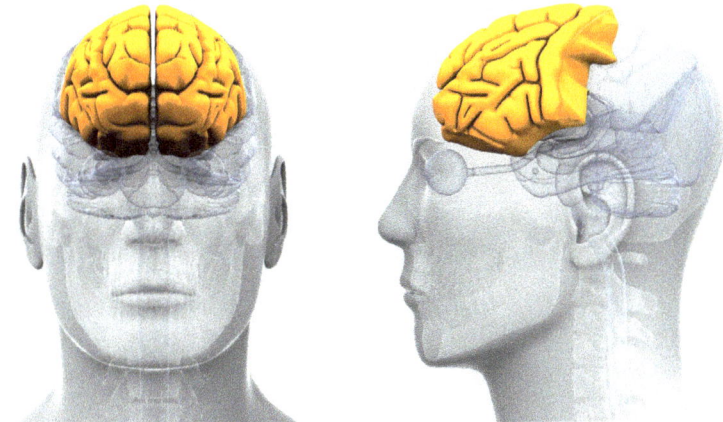

Figure 2
Frontal lobe

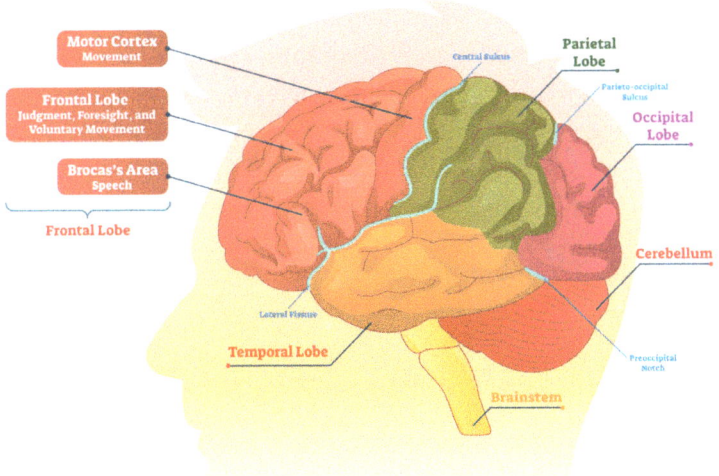

Figure 3
Frontal lobe

The top portion of the brain is the neocortex. By the age of seven, this part of the brain is responsible for abstract thinking, language, the ability to sit still, and connection with others.[1] The neocortex, which is shown below in figure 4, has the ability to take in and process copious amounts of information and apply meaning to it.[1] As shown in figures 2 and 3 above, the frontal lobe, which makes up a major portion of the neocortex, helps us to imagine future scenarios while keeping in mind the consequences that are shaped by those choices. It also gives people the ability to empathize with others.[1]

The prefrontal cortex is the front part of the frontal lobe. Think of your forehead area if I'm losing you already! It operates as a manager. The prefrontal cortex assists with impulse control and executive functioning. It manages behavior, emotions, and thoughts. The prefrontal cortex helps us figure out if a situation is safe or not.

Trauma can cause the signals in this area to weaken, which can cause negative emotions from a traumatic memory and hijack the prefrontal cortex's ability to reason. The prefrontal cortex shrinks when someone experiences trauma. The logical brain, which is on the left side, goes offline and everything else is a felt experience, which is processed by the right side of the brain. That's why after a traumatic experience, it's difficult for someone to remember all the details of that experience. Usually their memory is fragmented, and later on, bits and pieces of that event will eventually come back to them.

Brain evolution

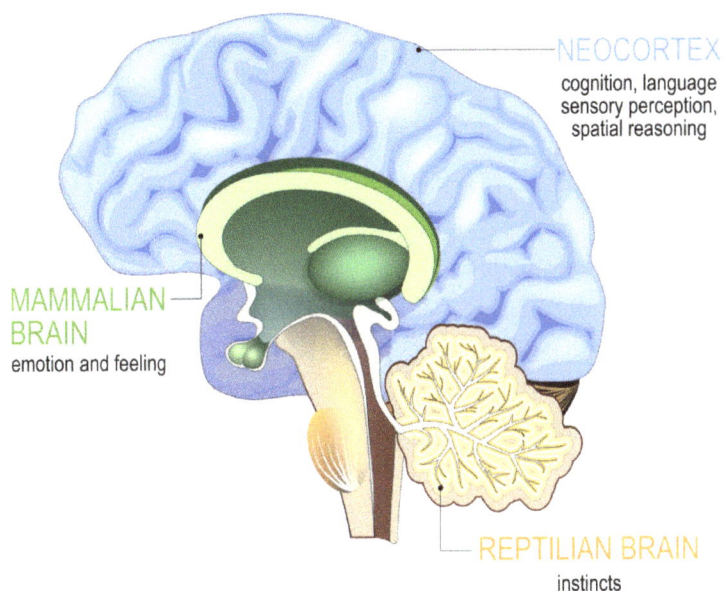

Figure 4
Three-part brain image

According to K. Cherry, explicit memory and implicit memory are two types of long-term memory, but explicit memory involves things that we can consciously recall, like our name, age, and rehearsed material, whereas implicit memory involves things that we unconsciously remember with little to no effort.[3] An example of an implicit memory is driving your car for the millionth time. It is something you do constantly that requires little to no memory recall.

Another example of implicit memory is that if your mother had you at a young age and didn't spend a lot of time with you as a baby and handed that responsibility over to your grandmother, you could possibly be holding on to the implicit memories of abandonment and rejection. You were just a baby, it's not like you could've rationalized your mother's behavior, but even as an infant, you felt the disconnect in your body of not having your mother around to nurture, soothe, and mirror emotions with you. So years later, now that you're married, if your husband stays out late to hang out with the guys and doesn't fully communicate how long he'll be gone, those implicit memories of feeling abandoned as a baby can activate internally and trigger you. Trauma can negatively alter a person's connection to themselves and others based on their brain's response to the implicit and explicit memories that are stored in their nervous system. Unresolved trauma is felt directly in the body as an implicit memory or unconscious memory.

The maladaptive memories that are stored in someone's unconscious brain need to be processed in order for that individual to feel a sense of safety and connection with themselves and others. When you're traumatized, your mind articulates a phenomenon as narratives and timelines, and your body articulates that same story as sensations and impulses. The term for this is *interoception*, which is your physical awareness of your body in order to help you identify your feelings, triggers, and emotions. Being aware or conscious of the sensory information from your body that's being fed into your central nervous system, either every now and then or on a continuous basis, is not required for interoception.[4] Oliver Cameron (2001) stated that interoception will influence your behavior, brain function, sense of self, and conscious experience.[4] So could it be that your body may have been trying to communicate your trauma responses to your mind all along, but due to the disconnect caused by trauma, the mind lacks the capacity to fully articulate what's taking place? If you're struggling with anxiety, depression, or any other trauma response, you feel it first physically before noticing it cognitively. The question is, are you aware of what's taking place physically in your body? There's a myriad of reasons why these physical sensations can go unnoticed, from dissociating to not having the necessary coping skills to regulate your emotions and thoughts in order to notice what's going on internally. By the way, dissociation is the distance our brain creates to cope with our trauma. I'll explain this later in chapter 4.

The hippocampus part of the brain helps with remembering things, learning, memory storage, and recognizing a sense of safety and danger. The hippocampus is responsible for calming your amygdala, which can be found in the limbic system section of the brain. Earlier, I mentioned that the limbic system sits on top of the reptilian brain, which is the middle part of the brain. When someone experiences trauma, the hippocampus shrinks in size. This, in turn, will hinder the signals that are meant to calm your amygdala. The hippocampus will transition from filing memories to helping your body pump cortisol. Cortisol is the stress hormone that our bodies produce, which prevents us from feeling much of anything in order to focus on survival. For example, if a man's arm was severely cut as a result of a bad car accident and he had to walk with his partially amputated arm in order to get some help, he would immediately start producing high levels of cortisol in his body to assist him in surviving this horrific experience. It's actually your body's way of helping you to survive a physically traumatic ordeal.

When the human brain is impacted by trauma, it can experience sensations such as fear and restlessness that can come alive throughout someone's body. After a traumatic episode, the autonomic nervous system will communicate a sense of misdirection, fear, and chaos to the body. The autonomic nervous system, which is displayed below in figure 5, helps to control a vast array of the body's involuntary functions that includes core temperature, blood pressure, gastrointestinal function, sexual function, and responses that arise in moments of danger and threats.[5a,5b] The autonomic nervous system operates involuntarily and doesn't require any cognitive thinking on our part in order to function effectively.

In order not to get lost in all the complex wording, I'll use the initials ANS for autonomic nervous system, SNS for sympathetic nervous system, and PNS for parasympathetic nervous system. The

ANS contains two parts: the PNS, which controls the body's capacity to feel a sense of rest and safety, and the SNS, which controls the body's "fight or flight" response and initiates the mobilization of the body's physiological resources to help prepare for physical responses to threats.[6]

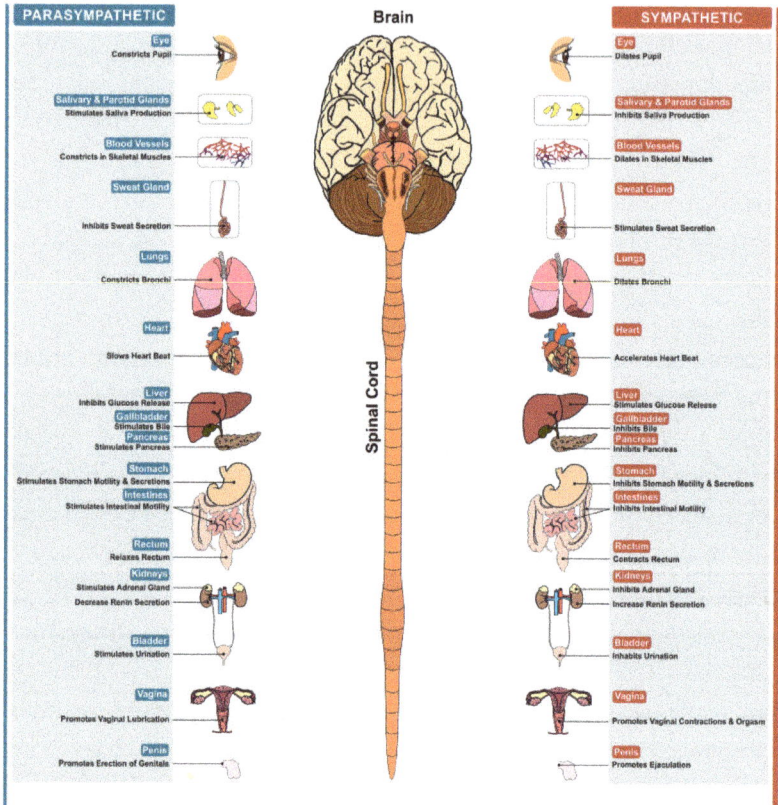

Figure 5
Autonomic nervous system

The PNS, which is displayed above in figure 5, oversees the "rest and digest" and "feed and breed" responses, which help return the body to a state of rest and cultivate growth and restoration.[6] Polyvagal theory emphatically states that someone's physiological state will determine a wide range of social behaviors and their ability to regulate their emotions.[7] The SNS, which is also displayed above in figure 5, activates the body's response to threat and lack of safety and connection. The ANS can provide insight into how and when someone responds to certain stressors that may manifest.[8] The autonomic nervous system is pivotal in helping us to understand how trauma manifests both biologically and psychologically.[9]

The ANS works hand in hand with the vagus nerve. The vagus nerve, which is shown in figure 6, is the tenth of the twelve cranial nerves leading from the brain stem throughout the body. It is the main nerve of the PNS portion of the ANS. The vagus nerve helps to regulate your heart rate, digestion, and immune system.[10] These functions are involuntary, just like the ANS, and aren't consciously controlled. After a traumatic event, the vagus nerve loses its ability to stimulate the nervous system to help it return to its parasympathetic state, or relaxed state. Trauma modalities, such as sensorimotor exercises, polyvagal theory, EMDR therapy, internal family systems (IFS) therapy, parts work, brainspotting, and many other whole-body experiences can help stimulate someone's vagus nerve to help them relax and calm down. The vagus nerve runs throughout your lungs and gut, and some scientists have even mentioned that it's a direct link from the brain to the gut; that's why trauma is a felt experience that initially starts in the brain and is felt throughout the body.

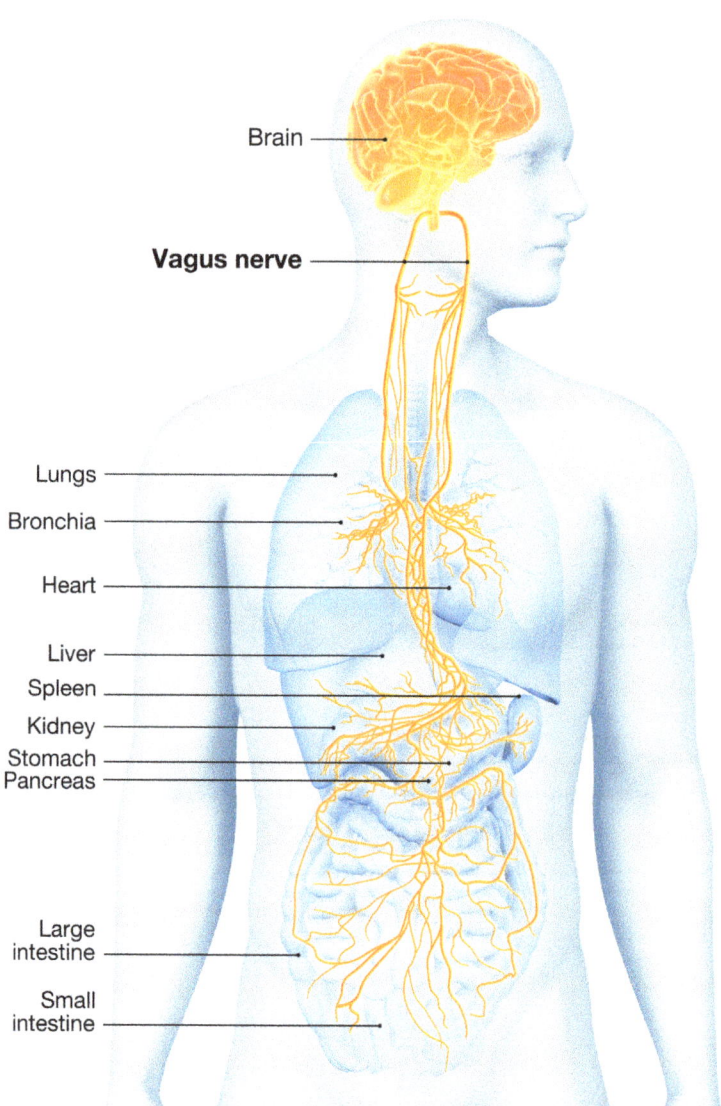

Figure 6
Vagus nerve

When someone's brain is impacted by trauma, the trauma mainly affects the lower region of the brain, which is the brain stem (reptilian brain) and the limbic system. Trauma therapy focuses on a bottom-up approach, which is first felt somatically (physically in the body) where the trauma is felt and stored in your nervous system. Traditional talk therapy mainly impacts the prefrontal cortex, which is our thinking brain. Talk therapy has a top-down approach, which only affects the cognitive or logical part of the brain. The trauma is not stored there; the lower part of the brain, or the emotional brain, is where the trauma is stored and connects with your vagus nerve and ANS. That's why traditional talk therapy cannot fully engage the traumatized parts of the brain. Trauma modalities that connect to the felt experience of the individual are what will help the body to metabolize or clear the stored trauma in the nervous system.

I was in the middle of my summer break heading into my seventh-grade year, circa 1993, to be exact. My parents and some of the parents of my friends in the neighborhood didn't mind turning off their air conditioner in hopes of saving on their electrical bill. The only problem was, it was ninety-plus degrees outside, and even if you stood under the mango tree in our backyard, you could still feel the sweat falling down your back. As I was heading outside, our house phone rang, and my mom's younger brother was on the other line screaming in Creole that their younger sister was dead! At first I couldn't make out the names of who he was referring to because I referred to these individuals as Uncle and Aunty. I told my uncle to hold on and walked outside to the backyard, where Mom and a friend of hers were hanging out and talking about things I had little to no interest in.

I can remember hearing my mother scream in distress as she rushed into the house to speak to her younger brother. I was confused and didn't fully understand the magnitude of what was happening or how to comfort my mom at that moment. It was heartbreaking to see my mother so broken and distraught. She was beyond comforting. I later learned that her younger sister was involved in a murder-suicide. My aunt's husband murdered her and then hanged himself immediately after. What was even more traumatizing was that when their kids, my cousins, woke up the following morning, they witnessed the aftermath of what had taken place in the wee hours of the night.

Years later, I started to better understand why my mother struggled to trust others and did not feel safe enough to even take a vacation. This particular experience, coupled with various other traumatic things, caused her to fear the world. I wish I could end this story by saying my mother saw a trauma therapist and is now doing well, but unfortunately that's not the case. There are some cultural stigmas from my mother's generation that cause her to feel ashamed about seeing a therapist and talking to a random stranger about some of her darkest experiences. I will dive more into the stigmas around mental health later on in this book.

Although two decades have passed, I can't even fathom how my cousins, mother, and extended family members are still struggling to make sense of this loss and brokenness. All of the aforementioned individuals will forever be changed and impacted by this horrific phenomenon. Out of respect for their privacy, I will not go into details about where they're currently at in life, but what I can say, even years later, is that I feel like I'm only now beginning to understand and process what really happened to my mother, cousins, and other family members.

Chapter Takeaways

Trauma affects the brain and nervous system and is felt throughout your body.

Safety and reconnection are needed when healing from unresolved trauma.

Trauma is stored in the nervous system, and that's why talk therapy is ineffective for traumatized individuals.

A traumatized person's body is constantly sending them signals telling them that they're not safe. The mind processes these same narratives as timelines and events, and the body processes these situations as impulses and sensations. The body truly does keep a score of all the horrific and heartbreaking things it's gone through or sometimes never got to experience. You can't just overlook these events and assume that they are behind you because some time has passed. Real trauma therapy consists of having to go back and face the trauma(s) that you have probably worked so hard to forget. I'm always amazed at the stories I hear of people going through some of life's most difficult moments. What I've found even more astonishing is the plethora of ways people have learned to dissociate and create distance from their traumatic experiences.

Chapter 4—
Survival Mode: Learning to Survive Hard Times

Bill is a retired widow who is well loved by many in our neighborhood. Every morning I would see Bill slowly circling around the block in his sedan with one hand at ten o'clock and the other hand at two o'clock, and he would repeat this for over an hour. One morning, I asked another neighbor, "Why does he drive so slowly like this every morning?"

My neighbor said sadly, "Bill recently lost his wife, and what brings him a little bit of joy is watching the ducks interact with each other."

*M*anny lost his wife after thirty-six years of marriage due to health complications. When Manny came to me for therapy just three months after his loss, he seemed distraught and empty. He and his wife had endured some tumultuous times together. Although Manny was processing his grief with me while engaging in EMDR therapy, I made sure to allot as much time as needed during our session so that he could reminisce about his wife's accomplishments and their time spent together.

Manny and his wife had been able to successfully survive the ebbs and flows of what would typically take out a lot of marriages. They made up in their resolve to remain committed to each other and their marriage in spite of it all. Over the course of therapy, Manny mentioned how he and his wife successfully built a thriving business together from the ground up, she authored several books, and she helped Manny to enjoy the simple but meaningful things in life, like family, quality time, rest, and the arts. Manny's wife was the quintessence of what it meant to be the matriarch of a family.

Early on, Manny struggled to grieve due to his constant concern for his adult children. He wasn't sure if they were creating margins in their lives to process the loss of their mother. In some ironic way, the loss of their mother allowed Manny's two adult children to be more intentional in flying in a lot more to spend some quality time with their father. Manny is now in a much better place after losing his wife. EMDR has cleared the negative beliefs of guilt and regret that tend to follow the bereaved. He's learned to perceive grief not as something you get over but as something that becomes that houseguest who follows you everywhere, and you eventually get to a place of accepting this new member of the family as one of your own. Grief gets easier, but acceptance of it will never fully erase the somber presence of losing a loved one. Some days are still a struggle for Manny, but for the most part, he's doing well. He has a solid support system along with his adult children, who still visit him every couple of months. Manny stated, "I miss her every day, but

I'm thankful for the precious time we had together. I think this is what she would have wanted—to see me healed and enjoying life despite losing her."

During the final year of my counseling master's program, I started interning with the mobile crisis unit. Two months into my internship, our unit received a call regarding a murder-suicide. The call came early that morning at 9:00 a.m. Another lead therapist and I arrived on the scene and interviewed the victim's older brother.

In hindsight, I wish there was a way for our department to simply send our condolences and schedule a follow-up interview with him and his family, maybe two weeks later. He wasn't ready, but we were there to provide immediate short-term crisis care to the best of our ability. The victim's older brother had a shell-shocked look on his face as he answered our questions. Apparently, his younger brother, who was residing at his parents' house with his longtime girlfriend, was involved in a very toxic and codependent dating relationship. They were having relationship struggles, and unfortunately, earlier that morning he shot his girlfriend as she slept next to him, then proceeded to take his own life right after. When I arrived on the scene, I couldn't help but think about my aunt and uncle's tragic situation from years prior. How does someone survive such a horrible ordeal without losing their sanity?

I'm a huge advocate of mental health and going to therapy, but I'm also a big cheerleader for someone's ability to persevere and push through their traumatic stress the best way they know how. Don't get me wrong, I'm not saying that all these different ways of dealing with trauma and stress are healthy and great best-practice tips, but I am saying that the will to survive in spite of it all is beautiful, even poetic. I have heard stories of wars, survivor's remorse, near-death experiences, abandoned children, tragic accidents, abuses of the worst kind, rejection, neglect, abandonment, and childhood traumas that have left many grappling with the effects of this well into adulthood. The sad truth is that many people will experience at least one life-threatening situation or violent event over the span of their life.[1]

Whether it's the loss of a loved one or a near-death experience, trauma can overwhelm even some of the most resilient people out there. Trauma is a universal experience that we will all encounter on some level, but we shouldn't ignore the marked individual nuances in the way people react to and cope with these traumatic events.[2] The human mind is complex as it is, and trauma can add to these layers of complexity. Some people will display very minimal symptoms after a traumatic event and return quickly to a state of equilibrium. Others will experience more acute reactions and will require a bit more time to return to their previous levels of functioning. Lastly, some trauma survivors will suffer from feelings of sadness for decades, ongoing intrusive thoughts, chronic stress, and a plethora of other debilitating issues.[3] Your ability to display resilience when dealing with unresolved trauma is a complex wonder that is impacted by several different factors. These factors can include things such as your support system, personality, and interpersonal connections and the type, severity, and duration of the stressor.[3]

One of the most common but interesting psychological responses for many trauma survivors is dissociation. Dissociation is a deficit in the integrative process of consciousness, memory, and identity that is usually connected to traumatic memories and experiences.[4] There are different types of dissociation. A dissociative client may look like someone all of sudden stopping midway through their speech during a session, staring into a void for minutes, and becoming unresponsive to what their therapist is saying at that moment.[4] Another example could be when a PTSD client starts to utter statements that are associated with an intrusive thought or image that surfaces in their consciousness and hinders the continuity of the previous conversation with the clinician.[4]

For instance, an adult individual may "fall silent in the middle of a sentence discussing loss or trauma, and then complete the sentence 20 seconds or more later, as if no time had passed."[5] The most extreme form of dissociation is dissociative identity disorder (DID). Clients who suffer from DID will typically display an alternate ego state during the session that accompanies childlike behaviors and speech if the traumatic memory is tied to child abuse, or sometimes an unfamiliar tone of voice of which the client has been unaware. Sometimes a client may display attitudes and beliefs that are incongruent to their personality.[4] DID typically accompanies more than one personality that has developed to help that particular client to survive the horrific experiences of their trauma.

No one decides to dissociate; this is the brain's way of protecting itself by disconnecting from its trauma and self. Dissociation will result in you discovering various parts of yourself that have been shaped and formed by your traumatic experience. The ultimate aim of therapy is not to get rid of these parts, because ironically they are still a part of you. The goal is to help you as an individual obtain a greater sense of safety and connection to yourself and the world. In doing so, your various dissociative parts, which were initially formed to help protect you, can now take a step back to allow your true and healed self the opportunity to take the lead in your healing journey. Imagine the horrors many people would have to endure if they didn't dissociate and there was an influx of all of the harmful and shameful things that they'd experienced personally or vicariously. It would be too overwhelming for most people to deal with. It is now clearly evident that dissociation, at both a neurobiological level and a psychological level, represents the earliest defense against traumatic affective states, and psychotherapy, especially trauma-informed psychotherapy, will help to address it.[6a–6e]

Real change takes time, especially if you've experienced a lot of childhood trauma. Be gracious with yourself. Real growth is measured in times of reflection, not while you're in the process of working through the worst parts of your trauma story. Don't wait until you've completed therapy before you celebrate the wins in your story. In the midst of the small milestone achievements, take a minute to pause, reflect, and give yourself a pat on the back, if there's no one else to, for your progress on your healing journey. When in trauma therapy, you truly can go from survival mode to thriving mode, but it's an arduous process that consists of clearing the trauma tension that's stored in your nervous system. Remember, many of the things you will work through in therapy weren't developed overnight.

As effective as EMDR is, and other trauma-informed modalities, it will still take some time to truly process the trauma, negative beliefs, and newfound sense of confidence in which you're now thriving with your mental health, especially if those traumas are from your early childhood years. Signs that you're healing are as follows: You're learning to appreciate the opportunities that you're given in life. You feel safer and more connected internally. You start to believe that you have value and worth. You're learning to trust others in spite of how scary that can be. You're mindfully noticing what's going on in your body and what's transpiring externally. You're no longer triggered, or not as much, and even when you are triggered, you're able to come to a place of resolution a lot quicker than before.

Your healing in trauma therapy will consist of a greater focus on resilience and learning to survive some of life's most difficult moments. Your trauma story's meaning changes as you heal, because you've gained a clearer perspective on yourself and others now that your past trauma is no longer interfering with your outlook on life.

I grew up with traditional Caribbean parents who believed in spankings. Although spankings are not at the heart of this story, it adds context to the lack of wiggle room I had when I got into trouble as a child. I know this is a bit of a taboo topic for some, so bear with me. I was the type of kid who questioned everything. I was very inquisitive, but that did not go over well with my mom. The way her mother raised her back in Haiti was to never question your parents or talk back to them when you were being scolded, even if they, as the adult, were wrong. Of course, I thought that was silly, so, like I mentioned earlier, I questioned just about everything. This became somewhat of a trigger for my mom, because it always led to her yelling at me with a lot of aggression. She would shame me by calling me names and cursing at me, very early on—as early as nine years old.

This became the norm, and I didn't think much of it, but later on, as I grew older, I noticed how offended I would get when someone would give me any type of constructive criticism. I also struggled to trust others and lacked a lot of confidence in myself. To add to this, I didn't have the type of parents who would hug me, apologize, or show any level of affection when I was emotionally dysregulated. As a result of this, I quickly learned to soothe myself, and very early on, I noticed that I stopped looking forward to spending time with my parents or needing anyone else's company, for that matter.

Once I became a therapist, I eventually realized that my attachment type was an avoidant attachment. I will delve more into attachment types in chapter 10 when I discuss healing that broken little boy or girl inside each of us. But for the sake of this story, an avoidant attachment is basically when someone develops a dismissive outlook on relationships, and the thought of emotional intimacy seems like a complete waste of time to them and makes them feel very uncomfortable. This attachment style caused me to struggle to connect to past girlfriends, my wife, my friends, and at times my children. Displaying any level of vulnerability or emotions was completely out of the question. I didn't know at the time that this experience led to me struggling with feelings of rejection and abandonment. It took going to therapy for me to realize that I didn't have the emotional capacity to properly nurture my loved ones or even to attune to my own emotional needs until I healed those childhood wounds. My avoidant attachment style also created distance between me and my mom as I got older.

Therapy helped me to properly place blame and let her know how unhealthy her verbal abuse was and how it affected me as I got older. Processing this with a trauma therapist also helped me to extend grace to my mom. I realized that she was mainly giving me what her mother had given her. I'm not condoning or excusing her behavior, but as I healed, I became a lot more curious about trauma, and compassion grew out of that, which helped to heal my *offense and hurt.* Parents need to understand that what they say and do to their kids may take them years to fully process in therapy as adults. Mom and I are in a much better place now.

Chapter Takeaways

The will to survive some of life's most horrific ordeals in spite of them is beautiful, even poetic.

No one decides to dissociate, but this is the brain's way of protecting itself by disconnecting from the traumatic experience and self.

Your trauma story's meaning changes as you heal, because you've gained a clearer perspective on yourself and others now that your past trauma is no longer interfering with your outlook on life.

The same way Bill observed the ducks in my neighborhood to help him make sense of his immense loss, trauma survivors are grieving as well. Grief is embedded into the fabric of everyone's trauma journey. You grieve the loss of what once was, what never was, and what you hope to one day get back. Trauma survivors are robbed of their childhood innocence, ability to connect relationally, safety, peace of mind, and emotional regulation. All of this and more will need to be processed with a trained and skilled clinician.

In order to effectively process your trauma, you must first move past the shame and stigma that's associated with mental health. Just about every culture and subculture has its own definition of mental health, and it's typically perceived negatively depending on the focus group at hand. I've seen so many people who are hurting remain stuck with their mental health illness and struggles because the shame of what others would think of them if they knew they were in therapy was too big an elephant in the room to ever address. It's sad and demoralizing for me as a clinician to see people suffer and remain stuck and overwhelmed with issues that could be addressed. In my opinion, it's the equivalent of refusing to see your doctor when dealing with a physical health crisis. Don't allow the stigma and shame of how mental health and mental illness is perceived in your cultural context to cause you to go it alone!

Chapter 5—
Stigmatized: The Shame Behind the Mental Health Discussion

"At the root of this dilemma is the way we view mental health in this country. Whether an illness affects your leg, your heart or your brain, it's still an illness, and there should be no distinction." —Michelle Obama[1]

*P*atrick was a down-to-earth kid who enjoyed hanging out with his friends and keeping an eye on his little sister. Patrick struggled early on to feel accepted at home and at school. During his middle-school years, there were moments when other students would verbally bully and challenge him in front of his classmates. He would usually feel disrespected but not respond from a place of anger or retribution. As a result of this, Patrick was shamed in front of his peers. He recalled having a classmate hit him, and by the time he attempted to retaliate, he and the other student were already separated. Patrick felt embarrassed and ashamed for not defending himself in front of his peers.

Patrick's parents had both come out of failed marriages, and they came together and had Patrick and his younger sibling. Patrick and his older sibling didn't have the same father. Patrick would often recall hearing his mother emasculate his father by reminding him that Patrick's older sibling was not his child, so there was only so much he could do to discipline this particular child. Patrick recalls seeing how broken and deflated that made his father, seeing how much he wanted to raise his stepson as if he was his own. Patrick's parents argued quite often, and his father gaslighted him by telling him that if he didn't attend a particular college after graduation or follow through with doing things his way, then he wasn't his son. Conversations like this made it difficult for Patrick to feel seen, heard, and validated by both of his parents. Patrick also recalls being sexually abused by a friend of the family, and he never spoke to anyone about this. Patrick's father's relationship with his stepson quickly deteriorated as he got older due to Patrick's mother's interference and resistance to making Patrick's father feel included in the parenting process.

Patrick excelled academically but never felt like he truly fit in with his family. He felt like a fraud around his friends and family because no one ever displayed vulnerability or felt safe to do so, so he didn't know how to truly express himself. Patrick abandoned *his authentic emotions in hopes of bonding emotionally with both parents. Everything felt like a performance to him. He never felt good enough and thought he was a burden to others. Patrick was naturally funny and intelligent, so it was easy for him to disguise his pain as comedy or to intellectualize most conversations.*

As Patrick got older, his childhood traumas started to interfere with his ability to truly connect with his wife. EMDR therapy started to peel back the layers of the different trauma responses that Patrick was exhibiting. He would go out of his way to please people or "fawn" in hopes of being validated and appreciated by others. This was to compensate for the lack of validation and secure attachment in his childhood. Patrick's nervous system was exhausted from making everyone around him happy while not attending to his own unmet emotional needs.

Patrick still has his moments when he feels dysregulated or triggered, but for the most part, he's learned how to advocate for himself by expressing his emotions. He has learned the power of being vulnerable around his wife, inner circle, and coworkers. After processing his unresolved trauma, Patrick is learning to find contentment in being present in the moment and to explore his emotions and triggers as opposed to being led by them.

There are a myriad of reasons why many people choose not to engage in therapy, let alone initiate the mental health conversation. Some choose not to address their mental health at all in fear of being ostracized by family members and friends or being perceived as being weak or crazy. If you grew up in a context that was permeated with survival, giving any level of attention to your mental health would not be high on the food chain. Sociologists Bruce Link and Jo Phelan stated that stigma includes a plethora of inaccurate irrational beliefs, negative attitudes, co-occurrence of stereotyping, labeling of differences, and consistently restricting separation and opportunities.[2]

If I took a randomized poll and asked various people groups to define mental health and mental illness for me, I think I would get a vast array of different responses. Could it be that we stigmatize mental health concerns based on our stereotypes, our fear of being shamed by our inner circle, and things we've probably seen growing up in some of our extended family members? If this is true, then stigma is more of a barrier than we may realize. The fear of being stigmatized for your mental health has become a barrier to treatment.[3]

Whenever I talk to someone about their mental health and their outlook on seeking help, there's usually a litany of things that seem to be barriers to beginning treatment. These barriers are things like the rising costs of mental healthcare, the fear of being labeled "crazy" by a therapist, and the fear of being misdiagnosed—and, even worse, being prescribed the wrong medication due to that misdiagnosis. Stigma may be more of a concern for African American populations, who are less willing to seek mental health treatment than some of their Caucasian counterparts.[4a–c]

Being that I'm a black man, I hear a lot of echoing themes within the black community of why focusing on mental health is not high on their priority list. Granted, the normalization of mental healthcare within the black community has gotten better, but there's still a lot of ongoing work that can be done to help foster a sense of normalcy and safety around seeking help from a trained clinician.

Psychoeducation, which combines educational information with therapeutic and experiential elements, may be one of the ways to address barriers to treatment and stigma against mental healthcare among African Americans.[5] Psychoeducation is beneficial to all people groups, but in cultures and subcultures where mental healthcare is not fully embraced, a psychoeducational approach can help to sift through the ignorance that helps to cultivate a culture of shame and stigma around therapy.

The premise of writing *Trauma Stories* was to deconstruct our culture's perspective on vulnerability. No one wants to be perceived as weak, and unfortunately there are many people who are looked upon as the go-to person for all things physical, emotional, mental, and spiritual in their families. Obviously, that's burdensome and unsustainable, and it can indirectly affect your motivation for wanting to address your own mental health concerns. Many cultures view strength as getting little to no rest and taking on more than you can handle, so burnout can quickly be erected as this deity that should be worshiped at the altar of *hustle culture*. If you're that individual, how can you ever muster up the courage to show that you have chinks in your emotional armor?

The stigma around mental health all stems from someone's childhood. Kids are shamed in so many different ways by their caregivers for expressing any level of emotional authenticity. That may look like being angry, so you throw a tantrum, and your parents could respond with "You better fix your face!" If you're sad, then you'll cry, and your parents will encourage you to stop. When children express these emotions without any reservations, their caregiver/parent will typically tell them statements such as, "You're crying over that?" "Come on now, big boys and big girls don't cry!" "Why are you so loud when you're upset? Why can't you be like your brother or sister? Look how quiet they are when they're upset." Statements like these communicate to children that their emotions and feelings are not safe here, and what child doesn't want to connect emotionally with their parents/caregivers?

Later on, in chapter 10, I will delve further into our need for a secure attachment to our caregivers, but trauma fractures that and forms insecure attachments that spill over into all of our adult relationships. Phil Borges provides commentary on this in a clip from Gabor Maté, who's a world renowned psychiatrist who speaks on trauma. He eloquently stated in one of his interviews that every child needs authenticity and a secure attachment.[6] If a child's needs are authenticity and a secure attachment, then when they're shamed for freely expressing their emotional needs, they will resort to abandoning their authentic expression in hopes of not losing that attachment and connection with their caregiver.

For example, if as a little boy my father sees me crying and says, "Boy, what are you doing? Men don't cry in this family," I will grow up and probably never cry again in hopes of not disappointing my father, whom I so desperately want to have a secure attachment relationship with. I've crucified my need to be authentic and freely express my feelings, thoughts, and emotions in childhood because somewhere along the way, I convinced myself that I would not receive my parents' love and affection if I continued to cry whenever I felt sad or hurt. No one ever said this to me, but because my father made those comments, my natural need for a secure attachment to my parents came into play and helped to form its own interpretation of this statement. I ended up losing a part of myself in childhood in hopes of not losing my connection to my caregivers. Now that I'm an adult, this may show up as me never displaying any level of vulnerability at all. Remember, my father shamed me when I last cried as a child, and I never want to have my emotional needs ignored like that again, so I made up my mind never to allow someone to see me freely express myself again.

Millions, rather, *billions* of people around the world carry this belief system, which causes them to view something like the need for help, especially mental health assistance, as weak and something that's not needed. The fear of "what others will think of me if they knew that I was even entertaining the idea of seeing a therapist" will be at the forefront of their minds. The stigma that seems to follow mental health around can be broken if each person is bold enough to admit that there are some things from childhood that have shaped their perspective on asking for help.

Earlier, I mentioned the need for psychoeducation, especially in minority communities. Psychoeducation will help you to work through some of the myths about therapy and barriers to treatment that can easily be resolved by a more in-depth perspective on the mental health discussion. A great example of this is simply educating many people, regardless of their cultural background, on the differences between mental health and mental illness. We all have mental health, the same way as we all have physical health. As we decide to take a more introspective look into where we are currently at with our mental health, we may start to find ourselves dealing with various mental illnesses.

Now, some may hear the phrase *mental illness* and automatically think it is associated with someone who's having a psychotic episode and is being involuntarily transported to a psychiatric facility. Sometimes that is the case, due to the severity of what's at play, but there are millions of people who have mental illnesses, and unless they say something about it, you would never know. However, a person who is living with a mental illness that is typically a bit more severe than other mental health disorders may display their symptoms in how they interact with others and in their various relationships.

The more education on mental health that is curated, the less people will carry around these skewed perspectives about mental health, what will happen in their first therapy session, or how therapy is only for the affluent or a particular cultural group. We tear down the stigma of mental illness one person at a time as we continue to cultivate a safe enough environment to keep these types of conversations going. The more it's talked about, the less therapy will be looked upon as something taboo or only for moments of crisis.

A couple of weeks after graduating high school, I attended a small album release party with some of my friends and cousins. I wasn't the type to attend these functions, being that I didn't have this grand affinity for music, but I decided to go anyway. I should've known something was off when we pulled up to the event. It looked like this little hole-in-the-wall nightclub. The place was standing room only with little to no room to maneuver around. The local artist who was the headliner of the show was the last act to perform that night, and I was so ready to go home.

As we were leaving, one of my cousin's friends, who doesn't need much information to go on to start fighting, said, "One of these boys just grabbed my girl's butt." I knew right then and there that this was not going to end well. Couple of seconds later, a big brawl broke out in the parking lot. I'm not going to lie, I wanted to make sure that the people I showed up with were okay, including my cousins, so I wasn't really focusing on who else was fighting. Next thing I knew, I saw one of the members of the group of guys that my cousins had had an altercation with heading to the trunk of his car and pulling out baseball bats to hand out to some of his friends. By this time, the parking lot looked like one of those bar fights from an 1800s Western film. This guy then proceeded to hit a guy who I wasn't acquainted with across the back of his head with the baseball bat. I thought he killed him. I grabbed both of my cousins and said, "We have to go now! They are swinging baseball bats!" Eventually they listened.

As we got into our car and drove off, I saw two more random guys get hit with baseball bats. About thirty seconds later, I saw multiple police vehicles and ambulances heading toward the scene of the brawl. I can remember looking at my hands and not being able to stop them from shaking. Mind you, I wasn't normally used to seeing this level of violence. I felt afraid and unsettled. I started thinking about the three random guys who were hit with the baseball bats. I wondered if they would be okay. I also started to think of how that could've been me; all of this because I decided to support some random local artist who I didn't even know. Explaining this one would not have gone well if I was injured. My cousins and I never spoke about that night, but shortly after, I decided to distance myself from them. I love them, but I couldn't afford to place myself in that type of situation again. I could've been seriously hurt or killed over some foolishness, I thought. It wasn't worth it. That night, along with several other traumatic events, was added to the list of stories that I would later process with my EMDR therapist. I now feel much safer at public functions, such as parties, but I'll admit, it took some time.

Chapter Takeaways

The fear of being stigmatized for your mental health has become a barrier to treatment.

The stigma around mental health all stems from someone's childhood.

> *Psychoeducation will help you to work through some of the myths about therapy and barriers to treatment that can easily be resolved by a more in-depth perspective on the mental health discussion.*

The stigma of mental illness is pervasive and socially acceptable. If you want to change the narrative about mental illness, you must first change the perspective from which you view it. What makes our minds so taboo and sacred compared with other areas of our human anatomy? Last time I checked, the legs, arms, neck, and internal organs are all connected to the brain. Most people won't have an issue with going to the doctor to deal with a physical ailment, but when it comes to dealing with their mental health, it's typically avoided or shunned. What would it look like if you began to normalize seeing your therapist like you would your doctor? Instead of "I can't make it this Monday because I have an appointment with my doctor," how about "I'm unavailable this Thursday at 3:00 p.m. because I have a therapy session at that time"?

I've heard so many testimonials about therapy, yet so many people are afraid to give therapy a chance. I used to be one of those people. Years into being a therapist, I still struggled with vulnerability and the willingness to do my own mental health work. I was a mental health hypocrite. I would not take the advice that I gave to many of my clients. Eventually I heard in different mental health circles about how other therapists were able to make incredible strides with their clients mainly because of doing their own work. This was what led me to, as explained in chapter 1, muster up the courage to walk into my therapist's office. I had no idea that this would be a defining moment in my life. I connected with EMDR therapy as if we were distant cousins. I was finally able to deeply exhale from my soul! Therapy was life-changing for me.

Chapter 6—
EMDR Therapy: A Deep Exhale

"The essence of trauma is that it is overwhelming, unbelievable, and unbearable. Each patient demands that we suspend our sense of what is normal and accept that we are dealing with a dual reality: the reality of a relatively secure and predictable present that lives side by side with a ruinous, ever-present past." —Bessel A. van der Kolk[1]

Simon's parents were divorced by the time he was in the second grade. Simon's mother was overly critical and would often remind Simon of how much he could never measure up to her expectations. This would be followed up with a barrage of disparaging comments and curse words toward Simon. He became acquainted with the following phrases: "Boy, you're so stupid!" "Come on, dumb dumb!" "Shut the f**k up!" "What are you crying for?" Simon quickly learned that the less he said, the better off he was. His mom would also gaslight him by making him feel inadequate for not following through with her instructions.

Simon's father took care of the disciplining. He used to physically abuse him whenever he got into trouble at school. Simon's father's method of disciplining was physical abuse. He would punch, push, kick, and call Simon all types of horrible names.

Simon's father was also very open about his dating life. Simon's uncle lived with his dad, and there were times when Simon's father would be engaging in sexual activities with his girlfriend and didn't mind having the doors opened, so either Simon or his uncle could observe what he was doing. Simon's uncle's and father's sexual exploits were quite intriguing and alluring to Simon. He was torn because he didn't feel safe around his father, but at the same time, his little eight-year-old psyche grew intoxicated with the types of behaviors that were going on at his father's house.

As a result of Simon's parents' abusive behavior, Simon struggled with self-confidence and the constant fear that something bad was on the horizon. Years later, he experienced panic attacks and severe anxiety, and he struggled with sex addiction in his adult years. His sex addiction led to him engaging in affairs that almost cost him his marriage.

Simon grappled with a lot of shame and wasn't sure if he could ever get past some of his most painful moments. When he started therapy with me, he processed a lot of his feelings of not being good enough and blaming himself for his parents' dysfunctional *behaviors. Simon also struggled with learning to identify who he was as a person apart from his anxiety. He had dealt with these debilitating symptoms for so long and was afraid of engaging with life without feeling anxious or uncertain.*

Simon is doing a lot better now, and his marriage is even stronger. He is now working in a field that enables him to be intentional about helping others. He still gets triggered every now and then but has learned to quickly recover and regulate his emotions without any assistance.

Before diving into my personal experience with EMDR therapy, let me first preface this by stating that EMDR therapy is not the only form of trauma therapy. I'm biased, and EMDR is my favorite, but of course I would be remiss if I didn't expound on the other forms of trauma modalities out there that have also helped others to process some of their darkest moments in life.

The following are other trauma modalities that I know to be effective in processing unresolved trauma: Flash Technique by Dr. Philip Manfield; somatic exercise therapy, which helps to heal you of the disconnect between your mind and your body and helps explain how your emotions can have an impact on your bodily reactions; mindfulness techniques; neurofeedback; brainspotting; Internal Family Systems (IFS) by Richard Schwartz; psychodrama therapy; and psychomotor therapy. There is a plethora of other modalities, but these are the ones that I feel most comfortable to vouch for and speak on personally.

EMDR is a structured therapy modality that is conducted by having the patient focus for brief periods on their traumatic experience while simultaneously engaging in bilateral stimulation (eye movements, shoulder taps, light bar, or audio), which helps to reduce the vividness and emotional disturbance connected with their trauma memory.[2] EMDR therapy is an evidence-based therapeutic modality, which means it has been extensively researched and can hold its own with all of the best vetted therapy models that are out there for helping patients heal from their unprocessed trauma.[2] The research supports positive reviews of how EMDR therapy has been beneficial in treating disorders such as obsessive-compulsive disorder (OCD), chronic pain, addictions, anxiety, depression, and other stressful life experiences.[3] No disrespect if you're currently on psychotropic medications, because I do believe there's a place for that if you've been properly assessed and given the necessary support along with therapy and healthy coping skills, but EMDR therapy has even been more effective than Prozac in treating trauma.[4] According to Francine Shapiro and Margot Forrest, more than seven million people have successfully completed EMDR and have experienced the benefits of this treatment modality with the help of 110,000 therapists in over 130 different countries since 2016.[5]

EMDR entails a structured set of procedures and protocols known as the adaptive information processing (AIP) model.[6] EMDR first came on the scene as just EMD back in 1987 as something that was helpful for patients who were battling PTSD, and then it developed into a more comprehensive approach known as EMDR.[7] EMDR was developed to be compatible with all major forms of mental health treatments as it relates to psychotherapy.[8] It follows a three-pronged approach, which means you're able to process past traumatic experiences, stressors, and triggers in the present and potential future events that may still feel disturbing. The AIP model, which helps to explain some of the rapid positive changes that take place during EMDR memory reprocessing, is the central focus in the brain to help promote healing.[9]

The AIP system helps to reduce the distress and negative emotions that are brought on by trauma and other stressful situations during an EMDR session, but ironically, trauma can also hinder the AIP system from fully taking effect. In other words, EMDR therapy helps to unlock the mind's natural healing ability.[10] Francine Shapiro, who is the originator of EMDR, stressed the importance of making sure that if someone is starting EMDR therapy, they are properly resourced. Resourcing includes relaxation tools that therapists can utilize to help their client work through the emotional and physical discomfort of an EMDR session. Clients can imagine a calming place or situation to help them relax during stressful moments throughout the therapeutic process.

If you are experiencing dissociation, your therapist should make sure to help you work through your dissociation enough that it doesn't hinder the EMDR process. I touched on dissociation in chapter 4, and it can sometimes lead to different traumatic parts that will hinder or inhibit you from proceeding effectively with your bilateral stimulation. Since trauma resides in the nervous system, during an EMDR session, you're likely to feel some physical discomfort at first, such as tension in your body, emotional overwhelm, and sometimes the fear of having to open up some old wounds. I've had some clients who were not ready to engage with a particular memory, and I had to assist them with expanding their window of tolerance. *Window of tolerance* means their ability to stay engaged with their particular trauma memory during an EMDR session.

In my own personal experience as an EMDR clinician, clients who've had a lot of childhood trauma and neglect will typically need some more time to work through the broken childhood attachment issues and distrust that formed during their early formative years. The positive effects of EMDR therapy will already work much faster than traditional talk therapy due to its ability to deal with the trauma that's stored in the deeper parts of the brain. So when I say that complex childhood traumatic issues may take a bit longer for someone to process, I don't mean more years, but maybe several more sessions. Everyone's EMDR journey is different, so there's no need to compare, because the AIP model in everyone's brain processes differently, but it will definitely process. There's no rhyme or reason to it; you just have to sit back and trust the process of helping to unlock the maladaptive memories that have left you feeling stuck and not thriving in life.

The therapist I first went to when trying out EMDR as a client didn't even follow the process with complete fidelity, but the benefits of it were still amazing. Once I got trained in it, I realized she had skipped a lot of steps in the eight phases of EMDR therapy, but for the most part, she was still able to help me reduce my disturbance levels in many of the traumatic experiences that I initially needed help with. I eventually connected with a more skilled therapist, and in the midst of all this,

I gained a greater respect for and understanding of this trauma modality. If I could experience relief from an EMDR therapist who didn't even seem committed to the process, what would have been the outcome if I had had a therapist who was passionate about my healing? This was a game changer for me in my practice.

I was amazed at how quickly my clients would process traumas such as sexual abuse, neglect, gaslighting, grief, abandonment, and rejection issues in as little as eight to twelve sessions, depending on whether what was being processed was an acute trauma, which is a single traumatic occurrence, or chronic trauma, which involves multiple incidents. I wanted every one of my clients to experience what I did after my first couple of sessions with my EMDR therapist, and essentially, that's what I've been on a mission to accomplish for these past couple of years.

Processing my childhood traumas felt like my soul finally exhaled for the first time. I started to better connect with myself and the people I came into contact with. As a clinician, I only have one speed in therapy, and that's the goal of seeing people go from barely surviving to thriving. Granted, this will look different for each individual client, but for the most part, progress is still possible and attainable if clients are willing to do the hard work of peeling back the different layers of their traumatic past.

I was twenty years old, and it was two days after Christmas. I told my mom that I was headed to Subway, which was about two blocks from our house. I remember checking the clock on our microwave, and it read 7:47 p.m. On my way there, I crossed this intersection that led to the back parking lot of a car dealership. Now, when I say back parking lot, it was very illuminated. So I don't want you to think I preferred to walk through dark alleys, like one of those victims in a horror flick who dies five minutes into the film. I walked past four guys who appeared to be getting into their car, but I didn't pay much attention to them. One of the guys looked like he was about fifteen years old. "Hey, man, let me holla at you right quick!" he said emphatically. I ignored him and kept walking and immediately heard him pull back the slide on his pistol. He repeated this statement a bit louder, but this time he started walking up to me as if he intended to shoot me. I initially thought about running, but the last thing I wanted to do was end up getting shot in the back like Morris Chestnut in Boyz n the Hood.

The teenager who pointed the gun at me repeatedly told me not to look at him, while his other three friends patted me down and robbed me. I put my hands up, and they took my cell phone, about $50 that was in my back pocket, my chain, and my watch. This felt surreal, as if it was not really happening. He placed the barrel of his pistol in the center of my forehead. "N***a, you already know what it is!" he stated tensely as he, along with his other three friends, jumped into their vehicle and drove off. As they were driving off, they threw my driver's license at me and took off. I later found out from the officer I filed the police report with that they were actually stealing the vehicle I saw them getting into right before they robbed me.

They say when you're about to die, your life flashes right before your eyes. That wasn't the case for me. My nervous system went into a freeze response as I stared at the barrel of his pistol pressed against my forehead and thought, I'm about to die! I ran to my neighbor's house and called the police. I could barely remember much of anything that transpired right before or after I got to my neighbor's house.

I would relive this near-death experience over and over again in my mind. Fifteen years later, while at a gas station, someone who seemed like he was in his early twenties had his right hand behind him and asked me several times, "Hey, man, what time is it?" Once again, I froze when I saw him put his hand behind his back. He was actually being courteous and was smoking a cigarette and didn't want to blow smoke in my face. As a trigger response, I froze. Right then and there, I knew I still wasn't over the traumatic *effects of being robbed years prior. I was bewildered at the thought of how I could possibly be experiencing the same exact sensations and feelings of fear as I did the night I was robbed at gunpoint.*

I processed this in EMDR therapy. I remember the level of discomfort I felt in my hands while holding on to the EMDR tappers that were given to me by my therapist. Trauma therapy helped me to leave the disturbance and fear from this experience in the past. I will always remember the details of that night, but the disturbance and negative beliefs from that night no longer control me.

Chapter Takeaways

EMDR therapy has been beneficial in treating disorders such as OCD, chronic pain, addictions, anxiety, depression, and other stressful life experiences.

Since trauma resides in the nervous system, during an EMDR session, you're likely to feel some physical discomfort at first, such as tension in your body, emotional overwhelm, and sometimes the fear of having to open up some old wounds.

Processing my childhood traumas felt like my soul finally exhaled for the first time.

Trauma leaves an indelible impression on you that can feel overwhelming and unbearable. The nuances and details of your stories may differ, but the various levels of adaptation to a threat can seem all too familiar. The intersectionality between the constant state of chaos and a felt sense of safety and connection will become more bearable as you resolve your trauma one memory at a time.

One of the things that can hinder someone from being open to the idea of seeing a therapist is the cultural acceptance of it. Being of Haitian descent, we were taught early on not to discuss our personal matters with people outside of our home. This is also a very popular sentiment in the African American community. It's not a healthy one, but it's one that must be addressed by taking a deeper look at how culture plays a pivotal role in engagement with therapy.

Chapter 7—
Trauma and Culture

Years ago, while completing my internship with the mobile crisis unit, another therapist and I were called out to a school where an African American girl had mentioned to her guidance counselor that she was struggling with suicidal thoughts and didn't want to live anymore. By the time we got to the school, the girl's mother had arrived. After I had assessed the child with my colleague to ensure she was safe, her mother pulled me to the side. "We don't struggle with this kind of stuff, so I don't know what these teachers are talking about!" she said matter-of-factly.

"Excuse me!" I said, surprised.

Theresa came from a pretty big family and recalls feeling a bit lost in the midst of all her siblings. Her mother displayed some level of emotional affirmation and attunement to her siblings, but for some reason she could never truly connect with Theresa. There were many different scenarios where her mother would gaslight her by making Theresa feel guilty if she didn't follow through with her requests. Theresa was also molested by a family member at a young age and never disclosed this to anyone.

Theresa's parents divorced when she was in elementary school. Her father remarried and was not as intentional in making time for him and Theresa to connect. This left a gaping hole in Theresa's sense of identity. For years, she longed for a little bit of quality time with her father but felt like his new wife was constantly vying for more of his attention in hopes that he would spend less time with his children.

Theresa's parents' separation left her with feelings of abandonment and rejection and a sense of being overlooked. She didn't feel seen or heard by either parent. Her mother would praise her older sister for her academic achievements and ignore Theresa's artistic creations and accomplishments, even her art school projects. Theresa struggled with distrust, confidence in herself, anxiety, and feeling unheard by just about everyone.

Theresa processed in EMDR therapy her irrational beliefs that she was a failure and unloved. Insecurity ran rampant in all of her relationships and friendships. Theresa is now a lot more secure in her friendships and family connections. Trauma therapy has helped her to no longer feel stuck in life. She can be present in the moment and not allow anxiety to control her. The biggest takeaway Theresa has gained from processing her trauma in EMDR therapy is learning how to give others the benefit of the doubt unless they've proved themselves to be unreliable and untrustworthy.

The traumatic experiences we go through as human beings are usually processed and filtered through cultural lenses that help to add language, which will in turn influence how we cope and subsequently adjust.[1a,1b] Culture plays a pivotal role in people's perceptions of the therapist–client relationship, their expectations of therapy, and even if they believe in therapy, for that matter.[2a,2b] We can't ignore the fact that current trauma modalities and their implications for treatment have been implemented by mostly English-speaking middle-class people and may not be culturally applicable to people from other socio-cultural backgrounds.[3a,3b]

Over the years, there have been growing concerns about people's basic assumptions about different psychosocial trauma models and how their various treatment implications are based mainly on middle-class white adults. A paradigm such as this tends to assume that people reside in what trauma gurus term a "benign universe" where traumatic situations barely occur and shouldn't be expected as typical life experiences.[4] The goal of any type of legitimate therapy is to help trauma survivors return to a pre-trauma level of functioning.[5] The problem with this notion is that there are people who have no context in their worldview of what a pre-trauma level of functioning even looks like. What if stress and trauma have always been your norm to the extent that you can't even fathom the idea of ever sitting down with a therapist to process anything? Stressors such as political, physical, economic, and religious tyranny could all dilute the idea of getting someone back to a pre-trauma level, especially in developing countries with very limited economic and political resources.[6a,6b]

In some cultures, traumatic experiences are looked on as a badge of honor and may actually add a certain degree of validation as opposed to violating someone's overall outlook on life.[7] If you were to remove this level of validation from someone who has tied this way of thinking into who they are as a person, then going to therapy is essentially the equivalent of snatching away everything that's familiar to them. Also, in many mental health circles in a Western context, it's not widely accepted to normalize the role of suffering in human development. If anything, therapy is utilized as a means to help put an end to one's suffering and reestablish a level of happiness in one's life. This perspective is counter-cultural to many non-Western people groups and religious beliefs that place a broad emphasis on the fact that people will inevitably suffer in order to attain a certain level of self and spiritual actualization.[8]

Typically, trauma survivors are perceived not as the cause of their trauma but as responsible for initiating their healing. A skilled therapist can help you to process your unresolved trauma and irrational beliefs by empowering you and teaching you new coping skills and strategies that can lead to finding new meanings in and perspectives on life. Getting to this level of equilibrium with your mental health will require the arduous task of walking through the dark corridors of things you've probably never shared with anyone. For some cultural groups, this can lead to a lot of anxiety and depression due to a lack of inner resources and the constant state of chaos and violence in which they continue to function on a daily basis. Alternate forms of healing modalities may be more beneficial and in line with cultural groups that do not have a framework that's in line with traditional mental health considerations.[9a,9b]

From the Western perspective on mental health, some incredible strides have been made in furthering the discussion, but within the American context is an eclectic melting pot of cultures and subcultures that all view mental health through different lenses. For instance, imagine you were raised within an environment where your caregivers taught you and your siblings, "What goes on in this house stays in this house." Well, if you haven't heard it from anyone before, let me be the first to tell you that this way of thinking is toxic and destructive. It will help to cultivate an environment where trauma can continue to be passed down intergenerationally, and the family name or reputation will be protected at the cost of you remaining traumatized and alone in your mental health plight.

Another example could be if you were raised in an environment where you had to learn quite early how to pull yourself up by your bootstraps, and it made you a better person. There's a lot of truth to this sentiment, but it can also raise mental barriers that convey the hidden message "If my struggles made me stronger, why would I ever want to seek a therapist for the very thing that helped me to become the person I am today?" My response to this would be to praise your resilience and how far you've come without much guidance, mentoring, or any level of professional support. This should actually be commended, but trauma doesn't always show up in loud, boisterous ways. It can show up in the responses we give when we display a little bit of passive-aggressive behavior when someone disappoints us, and instead of being honest about how they've hurt us, we smile and slowly start to emotionally moonwalk right out of their lives in order to protect ourselves.

Another example can be when our expectations of someone aren't met. How we feel about ourselves and the other person can be accompanied by past feelings of abuse, rejection, and lack of validation from our caregivers. I've mentioned several times already in this book that all logic goes out the window when we're triggered. So, to fully answer the question of why you should go to therapy, it's to help you navigate through all the emotional jiu jitsu you've grown used to displaying. It will also help you build deeper and more meaningful connections with yourself and others. Relationships and our outlook on life get much clearer and healthier when we can recognize what has and hasn't been conducive to our mental health.

Shame can't grow where there's transparency, and we need the safety to process and speak freely without the fear of being shamed for it but instead knowing we'll be validated. My heart breaks for those who've had to remain silent for years and sometimes even decades as a result of being groomed in a culture where trauma was widely accepted as normal and a sign of strength. This fallacy must be debunked by your willingness to become vulnerable with your story and the desire to make your mental health a priority.

In a podcast, Resmaa Menakem stated, "Many times trauma in a person decontextualized over time can look like personality. Trauma in a family decontextualized over time can look like family traits, trauma decontextualized in a people over time can look like culture and it takes time to slow it down so you can begin to discern what's what."[10] If that is true, maybe many of us are carrying around skewed perspectives on trauma, healing, and vulnerability as it relates overall to our mental health. Just because we've become numb to things getting better shouldn't make it right or acceptable for us to settle for the same cultural nuances that have held many of us captive, regardless of how much they're embraced in our particular cultural framework.

I'm convinced that a calm and settled nervous system and a mind and body that are in harmony with one another are what every culture and subculture should strive for. I don't want to be culturally insensitive and presume that everyone's healing needs to look like it derives from a Western context or from a particular international context, but genuine trauma healing means that toxic things within my family tree will stop with me. Intergenerational trauma is real, and I want to do my part to break its reproductive ability throughout my bloodline. I'm growing new and healthier roots that will help a new family tree to spring forth and bear rich and ripe fruit. I will get the help that I have so desperately longed for to ensure that my connection to myself and others will be affected for the betterment of all those around me. If you want to do something for the advancement of your culture, then take the necessary steps toward healing. It will be the hardest thing you've ever done but at the same time one of the most rewarding. It's worth it and so are you— regardless of your cultural background.

It was my junior year of high school, and my friend and I were driving to a McDonald's near his house. Well, technically we weren't in his car but his mother's car. About ten minutes into our drive, two police vehicles pulled us over, and an officer started speaking through his intercom: "Slowly step out of the vehicle with both of your hands up where I can see them." All of a sudden, another patrol car pulled up. We followed their instructions to a T, and then they proceeded to shove us to the ground and started screaming, "If you move, I'll blow your f***ing brains out. You hear me!" We were lying on our stomachs, and my immediate thought was, I'm being punked. This has got to be a joke, because we're not the type of kids to get in trouble with the law like this. The worst we did at that time was skip school to go play basketball and maybe head on over to the mall afterward.

They patted us down, and I overheard one of the officers say, "It's not them; let's head out." My friend started yelling at the officers and wanted to know why they'd pulled their guns on us, and they didn't even have the decency to say, "Sorry for the confusion." They just looked at us and drove off. From that day on, whenever a cop pulled me over, it felt like my heart sank down to the pit of my stomach. Typically, it would be for something as trivial as a speeding ticket, but that day as a teenager stuck with me for years after this particular encounter.

Chapter Takeaways

What if stress and trauma have always been your norm and identity and you couldn't ever fathom the idea of sitting down with a therapist to process anything?

My heart breaks for those who've had to remain silent for years, and sometimes even decades, as a result of being groomed in a culture where trauma was widely accepted as normal and a sign of strength.

I'm convinced that a calm and settled nervous system and a mind and body that are in harmony with one another are what every culture and subculture should strive for.

The cultural implications of mental illness can be very polarizing. On one hand you can feel like the concepts of mental health and mental illness don't even apply to you or your culture, and on the other hand you can feel like everything listed in the DSM-5 is applicable to you and your culture. Regardless of where you're at on the topic of your mental health perspective, it would do you a lot of good to gain a better understanding of how your culture has influenced your perspective on mental health.

The effects of trauma can feel like a raging chaos that will leave you feeling emotionally dysregulated, stagnated, and disconnected from just about everyone you truly care about. Trauma interrupts the organic flow of every relationship. Let's take a deeper look at this in the next chapter.

Chapter 8—
Fractured Connections: The Negative Effects of Trauma on Relationships

---

"Emotional connection is crucial to healing. In fact, trauma experts overwhelmingly agree that the best predictor of the impact of any trauma is not the severity of the event, but whether we can seek and take comfort from others." —Sue Johnson[1]

*K*evin's father passed away when he was only a baby. His mother worked long hours and left Kevin with many different relatives. These relatives included an aunt who would constantly beat and verbally abuse Kevin for some of the slightest mishaps, such as leaving his toys lying on the floor. Kevin's aunt had an adult son who lived with her, who would molest Kevin and sometimes stare at him when he took a shower. Kevin knew it was wrong, but he didn't feel comfortable telling his mother what was going on, and he certainly didn't feel comfortable telling his aunt!

Kevin's mom eventually moved to another part of town but continued to allow Kevin to be babysat by some of his other extended family members and at times by her church friends. Around the age of five, right before starting kindergarten, Kevin attended daycare. At his daycare, Kevin and the other kids were given recess time after lunch. On one particular occasion, Kevin was playing kickball with another little girl, and the ball rolled into the street. The little girl Kevin was playing with attempted to retrieve the ball and was suddenly hit by an oncoming car. She tragically died on impact, and Kevin and the other kids were quickly rushed back into the building as the daycare staff tried to attend to Kevin's classmate. Consequently, Kevin would go on to experience nightmares about this tragedy. These nightmares continued for years.

As Kevin matured, he struggled with feelings of anger and depression and was constantly hypervigilant, like a soldier who had come home from war. He didn't feel safe around new people and struggled to express his thoughts and emotions. Kevin struggled with suicidal thoughts and attempts. Thankfully, he was never successful with his attempts. By the time he came to sit down with me to work through his trauma, he wasn't getting enough sleep, and he struggled to connect with his wife and close friends. "I feel stuck, and I'm depressed most of the time," said Kevin.

Eventually, Kevin worked through his trauma and quickly began to display a lot more personality and vigor. He started to

> have a vision for the future and learned how to connect more with himself, his wife, and others. Kevin went from dissociating and feeling absolutely nothing to feeling all of the emotions he had learned to suppress as a child. Life wasn't perfect, but it started to feel a lot safer to him. He was very skeptical about EMDR therapy at first, but he warmed up to it by the third session. We built a rapport, and Kevin didn't feel the need to protect himself anymore. He finally got his life back.

There is a lot of research on the interpersonal effects of trauma. Although trauma can show up in many different relationship dynamics, most of the therapeutic treatment modalities for trauma survivors focus on the individual who experienced the traumatic event.[2] Unfortunately, there is limited research to evaluate the effectiveness of trauma treatment for families and couples.[3] When someone is traumatized, they have a lot of internal nuances to work through as part of the healing process. For instance, trauma is known to affect someone's ability to regulate their emotions and manage their close relationships.

Trauma survivors struggle to feel safe and connect with others. The disconnection caused by trauma starts with yourself, and if you're struggling to connect with yourself, that disconnect will show up in how you engage with your family members and friend circles.[4a,4b] We all know of someone who's struggled to sustain healthy friendships, and they're always at odds with their family members. How well you connect relationally with others, or how you've been shunned by others, can help you to measure the emotional health of your relationships. An example of this could be someone who consistently sees themselves as a victim. You have to walk on eggshells around this person in hopes of not triggering them. Maybe this person has been repeatedly hurt by those they've trusted. This could eventually lead to the traumatized individual feeling alone and having little to no support system, especially when attempting to work through past and current trauma. Like I mentioned earlier in this book, having a support system is crucial to your overall recovery. Having an authentic support system can help model the need for genuine human-to-human connection and a safe space in which to be vulnerable.

I know in an ideal world, everyone should find someone to connect with, but what do you do if you've had a history of being disappointed, overlooked, and hurt by people? Traumatic experiences can cause you to hold on to the negative belief that it's only a matter of time before everybody hurts you, people can't be trusted and aren't needed, and I've learned to do all that I need by myself. This sounds like a soapbox of strength, but these statements can sometimes mask themselves as wounds that we've appropriated into the cultural fabric of our lives. We all need somebody, especially when we're on our mental health journey. You don't heal or grow in isolation. That's why I believe that one of the worst forms of human torture is solitary confinement. To close someone off from all forms of human interaction is inhumane and can have some debilitating effects on their mental health.

If you don't have a support system at all, you can start your search by finding at least one person. Pay attention to all the different relational dynamics in your life—whether that's at your job or as part of a support group. Maybe you're affiliated with a local church, volunteer somewhere, or your hobbies involve other people. The goal of a support system should not be to replace your therapist but to provide you with a safe space to just be yourself and do life. Support systems remind you that you're part of an ecosystem that's so much bigger than just the individual struggles and stressors that you may still be grappling with. This ties right back to what I was saying at the beginning of this book. Once we realize the power of being vulnerable, your story needs to be heard outside of the framework of therapy. Remember, your story will encourage you and also those who hear how you've learned to navigate on your own and with therapy. I would encourage you to attempt to build a support system only if you feel safe enough to embark on this endeavor. I wouldn't recommend you start telling random strangers your trauma story without first building some level of trust and genuine connection with them. Relationships are forged in moments of vulnerability, authenticity, and relatability.

Having family support is vital to your trauma recovery.[5] Outside of your family connections, other forms of support systems will help you to reconnect with others again as you're healing.[6] Support systems thrive in environments where both parties are willing to be vulnerable. Many trauma survivors move in circles that involve a lot of people, but typically there's not much depth to those relationships. I'm not asking for you to find more associates but more people to build with and form deeper relational connections with. There was a study done on PTSD by Guay et al. (2006) that mentions that having that support system is an important ingredient in helping patients to fully treat their post-traumatic stress[7]—not only that social presence but also the quality of the environment that is being cultivated for your healing.[4a,4b] It's up to the clinician you're working with to ensure that you understand what a healthy support system looks like and how to find and cultivate one given the context of your situation. Sometimes, out of naivety and ignorance, you may think that your support system must come from your biological family, but this may cause further damage if your family dynamic is the source of your trauma. So your therapist has to be skilled enough to know what can be taken out and what can be added when building your support system.

Susan Johnson, in her book Emotionally Focused Couple Therapy with Trauma Survivors: Strengthening Attachment Bonds, defined trauma as an event that transpires:

> when a person is confronted with a threat to the physical integrity of self or another, a threat that overwhelms coping resources and evokes subjective responses of intense terror, helplessness, and horror (p.14).[8]

The stress brought on by trauma is seen as a mind–body condition that combines physiological and emotional responses.[9] Traumatic situations typically involve interpersonal disruptions, such as violence. Judith Herman, in her 1997 book Trauma and Recovery, refers to these trauma experiences as violations of human connection.[5] Your traumatic experiences don't have to include interpersonal violence, but quite often they can still evoke reactions of helplessness, terror, and fear.[10] If this has been your experience, you now probably maneuver through life believing that the world is a dangerous and unsafe place. Trauma survivors typically feel an immense sense of alienation and disconnection from the world as a result of not feeling safe within themselves and in the world.[2] If you don't feel safe internally and around others, forming and cultivating healthy relationships can appear scary and meaningless to you. True connection should start with sitting down with a skilled therapist, learning to become more aware of your body's responses to triggers, and lastly, connecting with those you come into contact with. Whether that connection is surface level or in depth, at the end of the day, it's still a type of relationship that you must learn to cultivate and honor. The various relationships we engage in help us to discern the level of impact and meaning we contribute to the world.

I grew up in a middle-class neighborhood that was safe, for the most part. The kids who lived around me were heavily involved in athletics. Basketball and football were the most watched and talked-about sports. If you weren't playing one of them, you weren't considered an athlete. I guess I was part of the generation of kids who still enjoyed going outside after school. Those are the benefits of growing up in the '80s and '90s, but I digress.

I got along with just about everyone in the neighborhood except Terry. Terry was a tall skinny kid. By the time Terry was in middle school, he was about six feet four. Me on the other hand, I was a cool four feet ten by the time I started middle school. Whenever I or a group of friends were playing sports around the neighborhood or just hanging out, Terry always had a sarcastic remark to say to me. I noticed this early on, but I didn't think too much of it.

One day while walking home from the store, Terry saw me and punched me in the chest, because apparently he was confronted by one of my older cousins who threatened to hurt him if he didn't leave me alone. Obviously, Terry was upset because my cousin had embarrassed him in front of his friends. I guess I was considered the lowest-hanging fruit, so Terry had to remind himself that he was no pushover by taking his frustrations out on the smallest sixth grader he could find in the neighborhood.

About a year later, Terry, my older brother, and some other friends were all playing outdoor basketball in the neighborhood when Terry got upset about a particular play and pushed me to the ground. Then he slapped my older brother when he tried to intervene. My brother picked up a metal pole, bashed Terry on his side, and chased him through an open field. That was the last time Terry ever bothered me.

You would have thought that I would have celebrated such a victory, but it actually shamed me. Although I was too small to ever physically win a fight against Terry, I felt ashamed and embarrassed that I couldn't stand up for myself. At a very young age, this event left me with a mindset that said, "I will never again be on the receiving end of anyone's disrespect." This became a major trigger for me as I got older. I was still dealing with what I thought was an anger problem as a young adult, when really it was just an unprocessed hurt that derived from being shamed in middle school. I processed a lot of childhood shame with my own EMDR therapist, whether it was directly related to something said or done by my parents or by someone I knew. Therapy helped me to learn to be curious about my reaction when something triggered me as opposed to solely feeling the need to react impulsively.

Chapter Takeaways

Having a genuine support system can help model the need for genuine human-to-human connection and a safe space in which to be vulnerable.

Support systems thrive in environments where both parties are willing to be vulnerable.

Relationships are forged in moments of vulnerability, authenticity, and relatability.

Unhealed trauma can be so menacing to the relational connections we attempt to cultivate with others. Trauma causes a rift between those connections and interrupts the intended plot of our lives. That is one of the reasons people are so quick to disregard their trauma story, because they've somehow convinced themselves that they deserve to be disregarded. Only an interruption in the intimate connections between your various relationships and storylines could cause you to dismiss your trauma, which is such an important part of what has shaped you as an individual. Your story in and of itself cannot heal you of your trauma, because trauma is stored in your nervous system. And the trauma that's stored in your nervous system must be cleared out by whatever particular trauma modality you're engaged in with your therapist. However, telling your story does initiate the healing journey for you.

Chapter 9—
The Healing Journey: What Healing Looks Like for Trauma Survivors

At first, I thought therapy alone would take care of my unresolved trauma issues. I soon discovered that it's more nuanced than that. On my journey toward healing, I've discovered the importance of learning to be present and embrace every moment with perspective and gratitude. This has played out in real time in the following ways for me: making time to pray; sitting in solitude in the morning; deep-tissue massages; appreciating the little things my trauma once stole from me, like the expectation that can be found in the dawn of a new day; appreciating art; laughing; traveling; working out; resting; being gracious with myself; and enjoying moments that I might never get back again. Healing isn't linear, but with the help of EMDR, mindfulness, and a dynamic support system it is definitely attainable, not only for me but for you, and also for every client who has entrusted me with their trauma story.

Monica was the oldest of four siblings. When she was in the fifth grade, she had a male relative move in with her family. Shortly after, this relative began to sexually abuse Monica when no one was around. This went on for some years, and Monica never disclosed this to anyone.

Meanwhile, Monica's parents had a tumultuous marriage and manipulated her into parenting her younger siblings throughout her middle and high school years. Monica coped with the stress of all this by dissociating, getting good grades in hopes of gaining her parents' approval, and becoming very busy with her school work and after-school activities. The stress of all this later led to Monica developing health issues and seeking love and affirmation from men who would use her.

In Monica's adult years, she struggled to set healthy boundaries with her parents and siblings. She felt a strong desire to be there for everyone by attempting to fix all their problems while abandoning her own needs. After years of suppressing her own emotions and needs, Monica didn't know how to show up for herself. She didn't want to be a burden to others, and she struggled to receive constructive criticism from close friends and extended family members due to the verbal onslaught she had received from her overly critical parents.

In therapy, Monica learned to give her husband and loved ones the benefit of the doubt in most situations. She's still on her healing journey, but she's discovered a greater sense of contentment in life and feels a lot safer and more connected in her body and with others. For years, Monica viewed sex as something disgusting and frightening. She later made the connection in therapy that this belief system was the result of the sexual abuse she had experienced as a child. Monica no longer sees herself as a victim but a survivor. She's passionate about using her artistic abilities to advocate for other little girls and young women who are still struggling to tell their stories and embark on their own transformation journey.

Healing from one's trauma is never linear and will look different for everybody. If we were to be honest with ourselves, many of us don't expect anything bad or terrifying to happen to us. We hear and see some of the most atrocious things happening around the world when we turn on the television, but at times, there may be this unspoken belief that events such as war, rape, and natural disasters don't really affect us here in North America as they do in other countries around the world.[1] Logically, we have a big enough sample size of our own disasters and tragedies here in America, but somehow many of us are surprised to hear of or to personally experience trauma and inconvenience.

I'm not saying that we should live our lives every day expecting to be traumatized or expecting the worst from people, but we should expect some level of adversity every now and then in life. Whether you realize it or not, trauma is an equal opportunist. I once heard someone say, "You're either going into a tough situation, in the middle of one, or coming out of one." If this is true, then what's the point of even healing? Let's just live it up today and wait to die in the midst of our misery, right? Not at all! The beauty of healing from your trauma is that you discover what it feels like to display resilience when stressful situations arise, and you also learn how to be present and find gratitude and enjoyment in just about every moment. The outflow of healing will be a greater peace of mind and internal awareness of yourself and your environment.

Earlier, in chapter 1, I briefly mentioned the term *neuroplasticity*. Neuroplasticity is basically our nervous system's ability to respond internally and externally to stimuli, which helps to reorganize its function, connection, and structure. Neuroplasticity takes place in response to your environment, learning, disease, and therapy, and such plasticity can be perceived as adaptive when it's tied to a gain in function.[2] Your brain has the ability to change and adapt to stressful situations. Certain neural pathways in your brain can be strengthened as new synapses are formed. Synapses are what connect the neurons in your brain. You have billions of neural pathways throughout your brain, which helps to connect one part of your nervous system to the next.

Think of neural pathways as billions of interstate highways throughout your brain. The synapses work like highway exits and on-ramps to help connect these neural pathways (highways) and help them to communicate with each other. Neuroplasticity is your brain's way of restoring the synapses that were damaged and/or helping your mind to form new neural connections to promote learning and healing. Neuroplasticity takes place when you're learning, healing from a traumatic brain injury, and engaging in physical therapy after experiencing something debilitating like a stroke. We are creatures of habit, so repetition really helps to positively influence neuroplasticity.

EMDR therapy is a great example of neuroplasticity. It's a repeated process that uses bilateral stimulation (eye movements) to help your mind form those new connections. You might not realize it, but many of us are actively engaged in neuroplasticity all the time, especially if we're constantly learning new things and are in therapy. Trauma alters the neural connections in your mind. That's why many of us will hold on to negative thoughts and beliefs that seem so logical to us, but when these things are noticed by others, they can appear very irrational and inappropriate. As you heal, you will notice the difference in how you feel and think. This is the result of neuroplasticity taking place in your brain.

In chapter 8, I discussed the need for establishing a shared connection with others, which is typically birthed out of relationships. Relationships are needed when healing. Therapy is just a facet of your healing experience. The more you learn about yourself on your healing journey, the stronger those relational connections become.

When's the last time you turned off all the noise and distraction in your life and sat somewhere in your home in complete silence? Not to isolate yourself but to embrace solitude. There's a big difference between the two. Solitude involves bringing into awareness what you've been avoiding about yourself. Isolation is usually driven by shame and your trauma response of not wanting to burden anyone with your problems. When in solitude you get a chance to slow down and pay more attention to the unsettling feeling in your body, whether that is your trauma, anxiety, or depression. This can be very uncomfortable at first, but over time it will give you a greater sense of agency over your unsettled nervous system.

What many people tend to do if they do not take the time to silence the chaos in their lives is remain overly busy with work, family, and other priorities. I'm sure you know of someone like this, or maybe I'm talking about you. Remaining busy will lead to a fear of slowing down and being alone. When you're left to yourself, you'll start to notice your dysregulated emotions, your irrational thoughts, and the bodily sensations that accompany these emotions and thoughts. Solitude in and of itself won't heal you of your trauma, but it's a component of your overall healing experience.

Throughout this book I've repeatedly mentioned how trauma resides in your nervous system. The next time you're triggered or feeling overwhelmed, take a deep breath and start to notice what's going on in your body. Maybe you're feeling a sense of heaviness in your chest, maybe your leg is a bit fidgety, maybe you have a slight migraine, or maybe you've noticed that you're clenching your jaw a bit intensely. Once you've figured out what's going on internally, I want you to sit with it for about thirty seconds to one minute. Get curious about your body's physical responses. Remember, you can't be curious and upset simultaneously. It's usually one or the other. Choose curiosity, as you're learning to slowly feel emotions and thoughts that have probably been suppressed since childhood. Becoming aware of what's going on internally is a form of mindfulness because it will help you to feel more present and grounded when feeling anxious or depressed. Grounding is having a sense of calmness and recalibration of your mind and body when you're feeling triggered.

Other mindfulness activities, such as journaling and deep breathing exercises, are so underrated. Many of my past clients are not fans of journaling. I guess it brings back nightmares of essay writing when they were in school! If you're in therapy or thinking about starting therapy, the most you'll engage with your therapist is either once a week, or maybe twice a week at most. When you journal, you feel like you've had an opportunity to vent and release a flood of emotions and thoughts that have been riding roughshod all through your mind. Journaling is so cathartic!

Deep breathing exercises will help to relax your autonomic nervous system. Earlier, in chapter 3, I discussed the two states of your nervous system, which are sympathetic and parasympathetic. Sympathetic is when you're in fight-or-flight mode and feeling triggered. Parasympathetic is when your nervous system is in rest-and-digest mode.

An example of deep breathing or controlled breathing exercises is "4, 7, 8." Learning how to first inhale air from your diaphragm will seem a little awkward at first, but if you're in therapy, your therapist can better assist you with how to inhale from your diaphragm. Try sitting upright with your mouth closed, and inhale through your nostrils for four seconds, hold it for seven seconds, and slowly exhale out of your mouth for eight seconds. This is just one of many different breathing variations that can help activate the parasympathetic state of your nervous system to help you feel calm and relaxed. If you were to do about ten of these breathing exercises daily, coupled with journaling, noticing what's going on in your body, and connecting with a trauma therapist, then you're well on your way to healing on some level. Of course there will be things to consider, depending on the disorder at hand and the level of care that is needed for your trauma. Your healing path will differ from the next person's, but the commonality of resilience, expecting the best out of life and others, and a settled nervous system will seem all too familiar to other trauma survivors who are on this healing journey with you.

There are many other ways to heal from your unresolved trauma that aren't mentioned in this chapter. I don't want you to think that I've laid out the blueprint on how to heal from trauma; I've simply listed some things you can do along with therapy to help you clear the trauma tension that's been stored in your body. I would also recommend dancing, exercising, and getting a deep-tissue massage every now and then, but only if you feel emotionally safe enough for this level of touch. If you have a history of sexual or physical assault, you may want to wait until you've first processed the abuse before starting your massages.

Embrace trauma therapy as well as whatever healthy coping skills you can utilize to help you become unstuck and enjoy life again.

*A*s a therapist, in order to show up well for my clients, I'm in therapy too. I remember processing an incident with my therapist that involved my father and me. For years, I thought I was a punctual person because of the time I spent in the military, but I soon discovered that this wasn't the case at all. It was a Sunday morning, I was taking too long to get ready for church, and my father was getting frustrated with me taking my time. Back then, as a ten-year-old, I had a mini afro. I remember my dad using one of those really big combs. Mind you, I didn't keep up with the proper hygiene of my hair. My scalp was very dry, and I probably only combed through my afro maybe once or twice a week at best. I can remember my dad taking that big comb and forcibly combing my hair as I screamed in pain. It lasted for probably a minute, but it felt like an eternity. I remember running my fingers over my scalp and noticing that I was bleeding a little.

When processing this scenario with my therapist, I realized that even as an adult, I was always on time and would get triggered when someone caused me to be late. This incident with my dad made me resent being late for fear of being shamed by it again. Ironically, it took me several decades to make this connection. My dad and I are in a much better place now. This was one of many different experiences that reminded me that even when parents mean well and are not trying to be malicious toward their kids, they can still say and do things that can be met with feelings of rejection and inadequacy in the mind of their child.

Chapter Takeaways

The beauty of healing from your trauma is that you discover what it feels like to display resilience when stressful situations arise, and you also learn how to be more present and find gratitude and enjoyment in just about every moment.

What many people tend to do if they are not taking the time to silence the chaos in their lives is to remain overly busy with work, family, and other priorities.

Your healing path will differ from the next person's, but the commonality of resilience, expecting the best out of life and others, and a settled nervous system will seem all too familiar to other trauma survivors who are on this healing journey with you.

If our earliest connection with our caregivers is as infants and involves our bodies, then that's where attention must first be given when processing trauma. Babies who develop secure attachments with their parents will cultivate a healthier outlook on themselves and the world. When trauma interrupts this connection, it manifests as distrust, emotional outbursts, fear, and abandonment (insecure attachment). Trauma survivors must learn to implement interoception, which is the art of noticing what's going on physically in their bodies when feeling dysregulated and triggered. You slowly begin to clear the trauma tension in your body as you notice it.

As you begin to heal, don't expect the patterns and details of your story to look synonymous with someone else's. Trauma healing will be a lifelong journey as opposed to a destination that says you never have to worry about getting triggered again. Resilience looks like the ability to recover much more efficiently and sooner than you could before you started therapy. Remember that growth is never measured in real time; it's measured as you reflect back on the changes and progress that you've made, so please don't forget to celebrate the little milestone achievements along the way on your healing endeavor.

Trauma therapy places a major emphasis on you providing a sense of safety and connection to that little boy or little girl inside of you. Trauma can be things that occurred in childhood, such as abuse, humiliation, gaslighting, neglect, and witnessing violence. Another part of trauma is the things you didn't receive, like loving attention, a secure connection with your caregivers/parents, provision for your basic needs, and being allowed to enjoy being a child free of repercussions. Having to grow up too soon by subduing your own needs for the benefit of adults has robbed you of intimate and precious moments in childhood that you'll never get back. You've healed and I've healed by our willingness to go back and process what was lost, stolen, and broken, mainly from childhood, in order to gain a greater sense of connection and resolve in our adulthood.

Chapter 10—
Broken Children: Helping to Heal the Traumatized Kid in Every Trauma Survivor

---

I never set out to become a therapist. At first, I was a middle school special education teacher for almost ten years, and many of my students were dealing with some of the most heartbreaking and challenging traumatic issues that you could imagine. At the time, some of my colleagues would pick my brain for advice, and I would give them my opinion and not think much of it. Later on, I became a bit more intrigued by my students' behavioral struggles and emotional dysregulation, especially if I had a chance to finally meet their parents/caregivers. After speaking to their parents, I was able to better understand the level of brokenness they were entrenched in.

Like I said, I had no intention of becoming a therapist, but a sign language interpreter who signed for one of my deaf students said on three different occasions, "Look, I hear how you interact with these kids, and I think you're in the wrong profession. You should seriously consider a career in counseling. You've really got a gift, Mr. Volmy." After hearing similar sentiments from several other colleagues, and with my interest in counseling growing, I finally decided to make the career change. What I didn't know was that I was already in a master class for counseling. My students were giving me a crash course on intergenerational trauma and how a holistic approach that involves individual trauma therapy, healthy coping skills, and an authentic support system is needed to fully heal.

Laila lived with both her mom and her dad until she was six years old. Her parents argued all the time, and on certain occasions, Laila's father would get physically aggressive with her mother. Laila and her mother eventually moved out, and Laila would see her father every couple of months or so. Her mother experienced PTSD symptoms as a result of the trauma from Laila's father, and also from other childhood incidents, which she never processed. Laila's mother was terrified of the world and would constantly remind Laila of how unsafe the world can be.

Shortly after her parents' separation, Laila developed severe anxiety and was diagnosed with OCD. She went to therapy, and it helped her learn to better manage her OCD diagnosis, but the anxiety would linger well into her adult years. Laila struggled with overexplaining herself and developed a strong desire to be accepted and liked by everyone.

Breakups on all levels devastated Laila, whether that breakup was romantic or the end of a close friendship. She feared the idea of not being involved with someone and also not having friends who truly appreciated her for herself with no strings attached. When Laila started therapy, there were a lot of buried emotions that she wasn't aware of, mainly due to her dissociation as a child. She had not yet dealt with the abandonment, with not seeing her father as much and suppressing her own emotional needs to ensure that everyone she deeply cared about was okay.

> *It took some time, but Laila started to process the manipulative and unhealthy expectations that were set up by both of her parents. With the help of EMDR therapy, a healthy support system, and continual self-care, Laila now feels a lot more secure and connected within herself. She is now more aware of her emotions, and when she feels triggered, she's no longer afraid to sit with her thoughts and emotions until they've subsided. Laila no longer feels the need to regularly attend therapy on a weekly basis, but she will check in with me every now and then to give me an update on how she's doing and what new adventures she's involved in. Laila is enjoying every moment to the fullest and credits a lot of that to therapy and her passion for wellness.*

There's a broken little boy or girl inside of just about every trauma survivor. Trauma therapists must first help their clients to go back in time to heal the unresolved childhood wounds that have not yet cleared from their nervous system. One of the most common misconceptions I often hear from others when educating them on trauma is that they have never experienced trauma and they had a great childhood. "That's awesome!" would typically be my response. I know it's a bit tongue in cheek, but stay with me as I delve a bit further. I begin by asking them follow-up questions: "Did you grow up with both parents? Did your parents/caregivers attune to your emotional needs as a child? Were your parents overly critical when you messed up? Were you given the opportunity to just be a kid and explore the world by asking inquisitive questions and playing? Were you shamed for expressing emotions, such as anger, sadness, and fear? Were you abandoned by one or both of your parents/caregivers as a child? Were you harmed or abused when you were younger?" Once I got the answers to these types of questions, they would follow up by telling me some of their present-day experiences and stressors. That's when our conversation would lead to a broader perspective on trauma.

I help people to better understand how past situations might have affected them. Remember, trauma isn't just the negative and horrific things that make you feel threatened and stuck; it can also be the absence of things you should have experienced. For example, when you cried as an infant or child, did someone pick you up and hug you? Did they hug you until you felt safe and secure enough to regulate your emotions? If not, this might have adversely affected your willingness to express fear, sadness, and a plethora of other emotions.

To add context to these conversations, I would find myself in situations where people would randomly spark a conversation with me out of nowhere, even if it was my first time meeting them. My wife would jokingly say that I must have a red neon sign on my forehead that says I'm a therapist. I don't randomly walk up to strangers and tell them they have unresolved trauma, but as we start to peel back the layers of their childhood, I help them see that it's been right in front of them this entire time. This is not only true in other people's lives but also in my own life. I have yet to meet someone who hasn't been impacted on some level by their childhood experiences.

We are all a culmination of all our experiences. Believe it or not, what you experienced as a child, whether good or bad, has had major implications on your present-day interactions with yourself and others. Most of our traumatic experiences can be traced back to family-of-origin issues. Family-of-origin issues include the different experiences and interactions you might have had with your primary caregivers and/or other immediate family members when you were younger. Your worldview has been shaped by how your parents/caregivers attuned to your emotional needs.

Attunement refers to how your parents responded to some of your most basic needs during infancy and childhood. Depending on your cultural background, your parent/caregiver might have responded well to your basic needs of shelter, food, and water but ignored your emotional needs. To better understand these relational dynamics, we need to develop a comprehensive understanding of attachment styles.

An attachment style is basically the emotional interaction between parent and child. This relational connection consists of care, pleasure, and comfort, for the most part.[1] In childhood, attachment styles primarily focus on how parents interact with their child, but in adulthood, attachment styles help describe the relational interactions and nuances in romantic relationships and also in friendships.[1] Attachment styles are broken down into two main categories: secure attachment and insecure attachment. A secure attachment is the healthy emotional connection between a child and their parents/caregivers. This consists of a healthy, nurturing connection between parents and children. Children who are scared will naturally seek comfort from their parents/caregivers.

Secure children will not turn away from their parents when they initiate a connection or simply want to say hello to them.[1] Children with a secure attachment will naturally respond to other people, but there will always be this special connection with their parents. When they see their parents, it's as if they light up with a sense of excitement and expectation. Parents of securely attached children are more responsive to their needs than those of children with insecure attachments. Also, children with secure attachments have parents who enjoy playing with them a lot more.[1] Play is a child's primary language. It's not like a child will cross their legs and say, "Mom and Dad, let me articulate my thoughts and feelings to you in a very detailed manner." Instead, a child's play and behavior is communicating harm or a sense of safety and connection within themselves and their parents. The research says that securely attached kids can express empathy a lot more during their later childhood years.[2] Securely attached children grow up to have trusting and long-lasting romantic relationships and positive self-esteem. Securely attached children also have the ability to better regulate their emotions.

Anxious-preoccupied attachment, or *ambivalent attachment*, is the first of three insecure attachment styles. Kids with an ambivalent attachment are not trusting of strangers and are considerably unsettled when separated from their caregivers. The irony is, when their parents return, they don't feel reassured by them. It's as if they don't trust their parents' return.[1] At times, children with ambivalent attachment might also reject their parents' attempts to comfort them when they're emotionally dysregulated. Their parents' inconsistent behavior in meeting their emotional needs is what leads to this particular attachment style.

In adulthood, someone with an ambivalent attachment style will hesitate to grow closer to their spouse and fear that their spouse doesn't truly care about them. This can cause a lot of issues in their relationship, including breakups and emotional distance.[1]

Breakups feel devastating to someone with an ambivalent attachment style. According to J. Cassidy and L.J. Berlin's 1994 article, adults with ambivalent attachment can become very clingy with their younger children in hopes of obtaining emotional security.[3] An emotionally needy parent can hinder their child from feeling seen and heard by them. A clingy parent can dismiss their child's concerns and passions because they're too focused on managing their own anxious attachment. This type of behavior is toxic and unhealthy, but unfortunately, most parents do not have the awareness and insight to perceive this.

The second insecure attachment style is *avoidant-dismissive attachment*. Children with an avoidant-dismissive attachment style will ignore their parents/caregivers. The avoidance magnifies as their parents' absence lingers. Children with an avoidant-dismissive attachment style grow emotionally apathetic toward their parents/caregivers. They could care less if their parents attune to their emotional needs or not. They also don't care to be comforted by their parents or initiate much interaction with them.[1] It's as if they perceive their parents/caregivers in the same manner as a stranger. When a caregiver/parent is unresponsive to their child's emotional needs or berates them for expressing their emotions, like crying, then this may lead to that particular child developing an avoidant-dismissive attachment style.

In adulthood, someone with an avoidant-dismissive attachment style will struggle with displaying intimacy in their romantic relationships and friendships.[4] There's minimal emotional expression in their relationships, and they experience little to no distress when their relationships come to an end.[1] Someone with an avoidant-dismissive attachment style may distance themselves from any level of intimacy by fantasizing about someone else during sexual intimacy with their spouse, or make excuses to avoid spending quality time with their spouse. This could look like either working long hours or running errands so as not to make much time for their spouse.[1] They don't know how to comfort and support their partner during stressful moments, and they struggle to articulate their emotions, feelings, and thoughts to their spouse.[1]

Lastly, the third insecure attachment style is *disorganized attachment* (fearful attachment). Children with a disorganized attachment style will at times display both an anxious attachment style and an avoidant attachment style. They don't have just one clear attachment style. They display a lot of resistance and avoidant behavior toward their parents/caregivers. Children with a disorganized attachment style (fearful attachment) will cry when their caregiver leaves the room and will continue to cry when their parents return. They are not easily soothed. There's a duality where they fear their parents, but at the same time they crave their parents' attunement and comfort.

Some of the parental behaviors that can lead to a child developing a disorganized attachment style are as follows: yelling at your child to stop crying loudly, making fun of your child's emotional distress, attempting to soothe them only to lose your patience and intimidate them in hopes of regulating their emotions, and being inconsistent in your response to their emotional needs. Another thing that can contribute to a child's disorganized attachment style is abuse. A child who has been harmed by their caregiver can develop this attachment style, and that includes all forms of abuse and unhealthy intimidation tactics. In adulthood, someone with a disorganized attachment style may struggle with depression and anxiety, negative self-perception, frequent emotional outbursts, and a desire to be in a secure and loving romantic relationship, but the idea of one also terrifies them.

Your attachment style will show up in your relational interactions and connections and in how safe you feel around others. Our need for attachment will continue until the day we die. The need for attachment doesn't all of a sudden disappear when you mature into adulthood. The context looks different, but it's still an emotional connection that everyone longs for. Everybody wants to feel like they matter and belong on some level. We're all somehow in a relational connection with other people, even if you perceive yourself to be a loner.

The imprint of trauma can rewire your brain to not feel safe in this world, to not feel connected to yourself and others, and to distrust other people. Your childhood experiences with your caregivers/parents heavily influenced those belief systems, along with the other experiences you had along the way. As you heal with the help of trauma therapy and find encouragement in sharing your story with others, you will notice how resilient that little boy or little girl inside of you will become. You will finally begin to process the lack of nurturing, lack of attunement, and whatever traumatic experiences you went through in your childhood. It will feel uncomfortable at first, but it will definitely be worth it when you can finally be present and engaged in your friendships and romantic relationships.

I was driving home from an event one night and it was raining. I had a 1991 green two-door Honda Accord and was not driving that fast on the highway as a result of needing new tires. I made a mental note to schedule an appointment the next day to have my tires replaced. About ten minutes into my drive, my steering wheel locked, and I lost control of the vehicle. My car hydroplaned and skidded across three different lanes on the highway. I started doing doughnuts with my vehicle like I was at the fair playing bumper cars. I was hit by four different cars at full speed. I thought I was going to die! My vehicle was totaled, and I could feel my body attempting to eject out of my car every single time one of those other four cars crashed into mine. Thank God I had my seat belt on. I doubt I would still be here to write this if I hadn't.

Three days later, I borrowed a friend's car, and I struggled to get back on the road. I remember forcing myself to drive again. I drove around my neighborhood well under the speed limit, and when I did get back on the highway, people were honking their horns as a result of how slowly I was driving. I didn't realize it at the time, but the fear of nearly dying was still stored in my mind and nervous system. Several weeks after my accident, the fear subsided, but I noticed that whenever I heard of an accident or thought of that night, I tensed up a bit. I ended up processing this event with my trauma therapist, and the phobia of getting into another car accident eventually left. I no longer have to deal with the intrusive thoughts of my car crashing into another vehicle or maybe worse, flipping over several times on the highway. Thankfully, that never happened, but the fear of it would come up randomly over the years until I finally decided to process the event in therapy.

Chapter Takeaways

Your worldview has been shaped by how your parents/caregivers attuned to your emotional needs.

Play is a child's primary language. It's not like a child will cross their legs and say, "Mom and Dad, let me articulate my thoughts and feelings to you in a very detailed manner."

We are all a culmination of all our experiences.

I never knew the journey of becoming a therapist would be ignited by the brokenness and heaviness I saw in so many of my former students' faces. The amount of trauma and the lack of healthy outlets that many kids struggle with is greatly disheartening. Many youths don't have the capacity or language to fully communicate what's really going on with their mental health. I can even say that many adults don't have this capacity either, let alone a child or adolescent. Children need to be reminded that their trauma story matters just as much as an adult's story matters. I felt called to the field of mental health to help push back against the intergenerational trauma that has been riding roughshod through different racial classes, ethnic groups, and socioeconomic levels.

Going to therapy can help break the cycle of broken kids growing up to become broken adults, who will raise broken kids who will consequently repeat the process all over again. One thing we can all agree on is that trauma isn't picky; it gets the best of us all. Whether you're on government assistance or living in a penthouse on South Beach, you can't escape the raging duality within that has been curated by trauma.

There is an ebb and flow with trauma therapy that can leave you feeling like you're well on your way toward healing, but there will be some days when you will feel like you're regressing. Regardless of where you're at, the main thing to remember is to continue pushing forward with therapy, healing communally with the support of others, enjoying life again, and pausing to rest and reflect. In the midst of it all, please don't forget to celebrate the milestone achievements—no matter how small they may seem to you. It will be the push needed to allow you to move forward and not throw in the towel. You've come so far!

Feeling emotionally overwhelmed and having uncontrollable visceral reactions and sensations will convince you that you'll never get better. The truth is, you're healing and failing simultaneously. The repetition of it all is leading to a more comprehensive version of yourself. Applaud the progress you've made thus far and be unapologetic about it! You still may have ways to go, but look how far you've come with your mental health.

Chapter 11—
Round of Applause: Taking a Moment to Celebrate Every Trauma Survivor

"Heal, so you don't have to give a sarcastic tone to uplifting messages. Heal, so you never have to make anyone else the object of your frustration. Heal, so when someone tells you they love you, you may allow yourself to believe them." —Taffy L. Gotora

*I*t was the summer of 2019, and my wife and I were expecting our second child. We were excited but nonetheless concerned. At the start of my wife's second trimester, her OB/GYN diagnosed her with preeclampsia. This is a condition that causes an expectant mother to experience high blood pressure. This was a little concerning to us because my wife has never had to worry about high blood pressure in the past. But we did notice that by the start of her second trimester, she was experiencing frequent headaches and a swollen ankle, which was probably a result of being pregnant and on her feet for too long.

On one particular Sunday morning, about a month before my wife's due date, I noticed that her stomach looked bigger than usual. I mentioned this to her, just to make her aware in case she felt like something wasn't right. By this time, we already had our bags packed in case she went into preterm labor.

A couple of days prior, we had recently had a new air conditioning unit installed, and the A/C repairman was scheduled to stop by to take another look at our newly installed unit. It was a Sunday morning, and I was heading to church, but my wife planned on staying home like she usually did and watching the church service online. That way she could stay off her feet and rest. As I was waiting for our A/C guy to arrive, I remember heading to the garage to grab something out of my car, and when I came back into our bedroom, my wife said frantically, "We have to go to the hospital right now!" I remember seeing blood everywhere. The hospital we were scheduled to deliver at was about fifteen minutes away, so I helped her into the car, threw the maternity bags in the back seat, and headed to the hospital.

I knew things were bad based on the amount of blood I recalled seeing on our bathroom floor. When we arrived at the hospital, I helped my wife out of the car and grabbed a wheelchair from the labor and delivery unit. My front passenger seat was saturated with blood. I informed the woman at the front desk that this was an emergency and we could deal with the particulars of signing in later. The other nurses and doctors at first weren't aware of just how serious this was, so I got the attention of one of the nurses and said, "Do you see all of this blood coming from my wife's wheelchair?"

"Oh my God!" said the nurse.

The next thing I knew, they quickly moved my wife onto a bed, and I remember counting nine different people surrounding her who had on either hospital scrubs or lab coats. One of the nurses informed me that they would have to do an emergency C-section because our baby was under duress.

They transported her to the operating room, and I was instructed to remain outside. Our baby girl came at 2:32 p.m. that afternoon, but I didn't hear a cry, which left me very disheartened. I feared the thought of losing both my wife and my newborn daughter all at once. A couple of minutes later, two nurses came out and quickly transported my daughter to another room, while saying a bunch of medical terms that went over my head. The neonatologist (NICU specialist) who helped to resuscitate our daughter came out to update me. He said, "Your daughter wasn't breathing on her own. I repeatedly tried to get her breathing, and at the last minute, we got a little something with the help of the ventilator, but I'll be honest with you, she was struggling to breathe for at least ten minutes." I appreciated his honesty, but this all seemed like a nightmare. I remember thinking, *This can't be real!*

Our baby girl was taken to the hospital's neonatal intensive care unit (NICU). Due to her birth complications, we were informed that she would have to be transported to another facility that specializes in more invasive NICU care. She also had to have a special procedure done called induced hypothermia. This involved significantly lowering her body temperature for seventy-two hours to help prevent brain damage. The tough part was going to see her. My wife and I were unable to hold or even touch our daughter. She was in this glass case with all of these wires poking and prodding her. I remember praying over her and seeing her move as if she *recognized my voice. Maybe all of those times of me reading to her while she was still in the womb are finally paying off, I thought.*

The doctors later informed us that my wife had experienced a placental abruption. A placental abruption is when the placenta separates or tears from the wall of the uterus, basically depriving our daughter of the oxygen and nutrients needed for survival. The transportation team from the other hospital arrived to transport our daughter to where they would be performing the induced hypothermia procedure. It was emotional for both my wife and me, since we were unable to hold our daughter and had to see her taken away in hopes of having some chance of survival.

I went home the following day to clean up all the blood on our bathroom floor. This is traumatizing, I thought. My wife and I later sat down with our therapist to process all this.

The induced hypothermia procedure eventually went well, and for the next four weeks we watched a miracle unfold right before our eyes as our baby girl recuperated. She is now three, going on four, and has no developmental or cognitive delays. Every now and then we'll look back over the photos of our daughter in the NICU and marvel in gratitude at just how much she has overcome.

Vulnerability is a superpower, but for many of you who have taken the time to read *Trauma Stories*, it can feel like kryptonite. I know I have a tall ask in inviting you to consider vulnerability as a strength when for most of your life it's been used against you to minimize, harm, and malign you. Vulnerability has also been used to convince you that you're less than and that you're responsible for all of the brokenness you've gone through in life. I don't want to dismiss how difficult and fearful vulnerability can be, but what if, along with therapy and everything else you're doing to heal, vulnerability is used as the spark to keep your desire for healing burning?

Trauma survivors should celebrate and be celebrated by others regardless of where they are on their healing journey. You've had to endure so much to get here. It's true what you've probably heard before: healing is a journey and not a destination. But if you don't come in with this mindset, you can get discouraged at the first sign of a trigger or disappointing moment in life. Welcome to the club! Perfection doesn't sit well with people who are learning to adapt to changes within and around them. The learning curve for trauma survivors is that you're applauding the fact that you're still here in spite of it all!

Vulnerability is at the center of meaningful communication. I'm referring to the freedom to express yourself without feeling the need to protect yourself from feeling ashamed or vulnerable. Whether we're referring to a romantic relationship or a friendship, vulnerability can help foster a certain level of freedom in a conversation that many trauma survivors have yet to experience. An example of this is saying, "I'm sorry," "I love you," "I was in the wrong," "Could you please help me?" "Thank you," "I don't have the answer to that question," "I was hurt," "I shouldn't have judged you," or "I'm afraid." Imagine the depths of freedom and connection our conversations would have if we cultivated a safe space to display this level of vulnerability with others. Don't get me wrong; it certainly takes a lot of emotional energy to communicate this level of vulnerability, but as you heal, you'll discover the strength behind this.

You have to make a conscious decision every day to continue to do the hard work of improving your mental health. Nothing is handed to you, and the discomfort that accompanies change can make you feel like maybe you made a mistake and should just accept fear, distrust, and a lack of emotional intelligence and fluency as your fate. Life will be hard regardless, but on the other side of hard is a place of emotional stability and gratitude. I won't sell you a clichéd story of your reason for going through whatever traumatic experience you went through. First of all, it's a bit inconsiderate, and second, I don't know all the nuances and dysfunctional situations you've had to deal with. You should be celebrated for your resolve that no matter what you have to go through to heal, it can't be as bad as what you've been tolerating with your unresolved trauma.

Maybe there's still an unhealed emotional wound telling you you're undeserving of rest or of a sense of mental clarity and wellness. You can't celebrate what you believe you don't deserve. Your mindset toward healing must change if you intend to process your trauma. Your decision to heal is not just for you but for the generations to come that will be affected for the better. Your healing will affect your personal life, your romantic relationships, your work life, your friendships, and your relationships with your extended family members. We will continue to repeat what we refuse to change, so you might as well be the cycle breaker of intergenerational trauma in your family's bloodline.

In the same way as trauma destroys relational connections, healing from your trauma helps to forge healthier relational connections. Trauma healing will help you gain a clearer perspective on your emotions and thoughts, which will in turn help you to better understand and connect with yourself and those around you. Trauma healing is a journey that consists of a collection of a thousand different moments that shouldn't be taken for granted. Trauma therapy just happens to be one of those moments. I know this may sound a bit blasphemous coming from a therapist, but therapy alone isn't all that's needed on your healing journey. It will take a collection of hugs and kisses from loved ones, encouraging text messages from friends, communal healing, support groups, mindfulness and relaxation activities, rest, trauma therapy, learning to be still, becoming aware of the physical sensations of your triggers, and so much more.

In most of the chapters in *Trauma Stories*, you probably noticed that I shared a personal story about myself and one from the life of a past client. I purposely didn't share another story from one of my past clients in this chapter, because I wanted to leave room for you to start yours. I feel like if you've made it this far in the book, I might as well consider you an honorary client. No, seriously, who's to say that there aren't others who are waiting to hear a story of survival, perseverance, and healing? Healing might as well come from someone who is peeling back the layers of unresolved trauma and attachment wounds and who desires to see others impacted positively by their journey. So why not start by telling your trauma story? Maybe you've never been told this before, but I see you, I hear you, and I applaud you on this journey toward mental wellness. The arduous task of ongoing trauma healing is not for the faint of heart. I celebrate you, whether you're at the start, in the middle, or near the end of getting to a healthier and more settled version of yourself. Thank you!

Chapter Takeaways

Healing from trauma is not a destination. It's a journey.

Trauma healing is a journey that consists of a collection of a thousand different moments that shouldn't be taken for granted. Trauma therapy just happens to be one of those moments.

You can't celebrate what you don't believe you deserve. Your mindset toward healing must change if you intend to process your trauma.

The traumatic stress and attachment wounds that many of you have suffered from can be so debilitating. You will never get to the core of your authentic self until you've processed the trauma tension that you've been storing in your body. I'm passionate about seeing the transformation that takes place when someone begins to share their story; becomes vulnerable; or engages in a trauma modality such as EMDR, internal family systems (IFS), mindfulness techniques, or somatic exercising. The more trauma tension that is released from your nervous system, the less you'll react to your triggers—the less you'll be controlled by the negative beliefs and emotions that have been lying to you for quite some time now. As countercultural as this might sound, your vulnerability in sharing your trauma story can be the catalyst needed to initiate your healing journey. Vulnerability will help lead you to a greater sense of relatability and connection with others who are still stuck, broken, and at their wits' end. I'm not saying that everyone who heals from their unresolved trauma is destined to become a future therapist, but you have no idea who will be inspired by the resilience in your story.

Conclusion

At the time of writing *Trauma Stories*, my daughters are ages three and seven. Sometimes I'll notice that they could use a helping hand from me. "I got it!" seems to be the usual response to my request to help them. I'll patiently wait for about another minute, and they'll follow up with, "Daddy, help me!" with a pinch of embarrassment in their tone. I make sure not to shame them by laughing or saying, "I told you so." I use these moments as lessons to remind them that we'll never outgrow our need for help from others. Believe it or not, we all need each other, and *Trauma Stories* was written as a long-winded response about how to teach our minds and bodies to ask for help in times of both crisis and prevention. Vulnerability is a strength that many refuse to lean on.

I hope the stories in this book are a reminder that you're not alone, your story matters, and you can actually heal and grow beyond where your trauma has held you captive. The visceral terror that accompanies trauma convinces many of you that you'll always be held captive by your fear. *Trauma Stories* is an introduction to what freedom looks like and the normalization of vulnerability.

Trauma Stories is about a therapist expounding on the power of vulnerability within our stories and how these stories matter and connect us. Your story matters because it connects people in different ways by utilizing vulnerability as an agent of change and healing. The more we normalize the conversation around therapy, the more we lessen the stigma attached to it. This stigma is rooted in shame of what others will think of you. Safety and reconnection are needed when healing from unresolved trauma. When in trauma therapy, you can go from survival mode to thriving mode. Mental health stigma varies between different ethnic groups and cultural backgrounds.

EMDR can help process unresolved trauma on a much deeper level than traditional talk therapy. There are ways in which different cultures express, experience, and cope with feelings of distress. It's important that trauma therapists explain how trauma affects individuals and their relational connections. Trauma survivors should learn to implement interoception, which is the art of noticing what's going on physically in their bodies. You slowly begin to clear the trauma tension in your body as you notice it. Trauma physically resides in the nervous system. There's a broken little boy or little girl inside of every trauma survivor. A skilled therapist has to first help their client go back in time to heal the childhood wounds that have not yet resolved. Trauma healing is a journey that consists of a thousand different moments that shouldn't be taken for granted. Trauma therapy just happens to be one of those moments.

You should take some time to process what you've just read and analyze how you perceive your own trauma story and journey. You may recall the various times throughout *Trauma Stories* when you read about the power of being vulnerable with your story and removing the stigma of connecting with a trauma therapist, preferably an EMDR therapist. You will see the power of normalizing the mental health conversation if you desire to evoke change within yourself and your sphere of influence.

Endnotes

Introduction
[1] Mental Health America, *The State of Mental Health in America* (Mental Health America, 2023), accessed February 17, 2023, at www.mhanational.org/issues/state-mental-health-america.

Chapter 1— Storytellers: Your Story Matters
[1] American Psychiatric Association, *Diagnostic and Statistical Manual of Mental Disorders (DSM-5)* (Arlington, VA: APA, 2013).

[2] B. A. van der Kolk, "Developmental Trauma Disorder," *Psychiatric Annals* 35, no. 5 (2005): 401–408. doi:10.3928/00485713-20050501-06.

Chapter 2— Office Hours: We All Need Therapy
[1] A. Gopaldas, "Therapy," *Consumption Markets and Culture* 19, no. 3 (2016): 264–268. doi:10.1080/10253866.2015.1096070.

[2] J. Engel, *American Therapy: The Rise of Psychotherapy in the United States* (New York: Penguin, 2008).

[3] A. Gopaldas, "Marketplace Sentiments," *Journal of Consumer Research* 41, no. 4 (2014): 995–1014. doi:10.1086/678034.

[4] E. Illouz, *Saving the Modern Soul: Therapy, Emotions, and the Culture of Self-Help* (Berkeley: University of California Press, 2008).

Chapter 3— Excuse Me! Trauma Affects the Mind and Body Differently?
[1] B. A. van der Kolk, *The Body Keeps the Score: Brain, Mind, and Body in the Healing of Trauma* (New York: Penguin).

[2] D. Servan-Schreiber, *The Instinct to Heal: Curing Stress, Anxiety, and Depression without Drugs and without Talk Therapy* (Emmaus, PA: Rodale Press, 2004).

[3] K. Cherry, "What's the Difference between Implicit and Explicit Memory?," *Verywell Mind* (2022), accessed March 4, 2023, at www.verywellmind.com/implicit-and-explicit-memory-2795346.

[4] O. G. Cameron, *Visceral Sensory Neuroscience: Interoception* (Oxford, UK: Oxford University Press, 2001).

5a C. H. Gibbons, "Basics of Autonomic Nervous System Function," *Handbook of Clinical Neurology* 160 (2019): 407–418. doi:10.1016/B978-0-444-64032-1.00027-8.

5b M. E. Kemeny, "The Psychobiology of Stress," *Current Directions in Psychological Science* 12, no. 4 (2003): 124–129. doi:10.1111/1467-8721.01246.

[6] L. K. McCorry, "Physiology of the Autonomic Nervous System," *American Journal of Pharmaceutical Education* 71, no. 4 (2007). doi:10.5688/aj710478.

[7] S. W. Porges, "The Polyvagal Perspective," *Biological Psychology* 74, no. 2 (2007): 116–143. doi:10.1016/j.biopsycho.2006.06.009.

[8] S. W. Porges, "The Polyvagal Theory: Phylogenetic Contributions to Social Behavior," *Physiology and Behavior* 79, no. 3 (2003): 503–513. doi:10.1016/s0031-9384(03)00156-2.

[9] R. E. Siciliano, A. S. Anderson, and B. E. Compas, "Autonomic Nervous System Correlates of Posttraumatic Stress Symptoms in Youth: Meta-analysis and Qualitative Review," *Clinical Psychology Review* 92 (2022): 102–125. doi:10.1016/j.cpr.2022.10212.

[10] V. A. Pavlov and K. J. Tracey, "The Vagus Nerve and the Inflammatory Reflex: Linking Immunity and Metabolism," *Nature Reviews Endocrinology* 8, no. 12 (2012): 743+. doi:10.1038/nrendo.2012.189.

Figure 1: Limbic system, including the amygdala (Adobe Stock Image # 401503443)

Figure 2: Frontal lobe (Adobe Stock Image # 74188334)

Figure 3: Frontal lobe (Adobe Stock Image # 227287282)

Figure 4: Three-part brain image (Adobe Stock Image # 256606272)

Figure 5: Autonomic nervous system (Adobe Stock Image # 504555354)

Figure 6: Vagus nerve (Adobe Stock Image # 540273348)

Chapter 4— Survival Mode: Learning to Survive Hard Times

[1] R. C. Kessler, A. Sonnega, E. Bromet, M. Hughes, and C. B. Nelson, "Posttraumatic Stress Disorder in the National Comorbidity Survey," *Archives of General Psychiatry* 52 (1995): 1048–1060. doi:10.1001/archpsyc.1995.03950240066012.

[2] G. A. Bonanno and S. Kaltman, "Toward an Integrative Perspective on Bereavement," *Psychological Bulletin* 125 (1999): 760–776. doi:10.1037/0033-2909.125.6.760. PMID: 10589301.

[3] G. A. Bonanno. "Resilience in the Face of Potential Trauma: Clinical Practices and Illustrations," *Journal of Clinical Psychology* 62, no. 8 (2006): 971–985. doi:10.1002/jclp.20283. PMID: 16700017.

[4] G. Liotti, "Trauma, Dissociation, and Disorganized Attachment: Three Strands of a Single Braid," *Psychotherapy: Theory, Research, Practice, Training* 41, no. 4 (2004): 472–486. doi:10.1037/0033-3204.41.4.472.

[5] M. Main and H. Morgan, "Disorganization and Disorientation in Infant Strange Situation Behavior: Phenotypic Resemblance to Dissociative States," in *Handbook of Dissociation: Theoretical, Empirical, and Clinical Perspectives*, ed. L. K. Michelson and W. J. Ray (Springer, 1996), 107–138.

[6a] C. Mucci, "Borderline Bodies: Affect Regulation Therapy for Personality Disorders," in *Norton Series on Interpersonal Neurobiology*, ed. L. Cozolino, A. N. Schore, and D. J. Siegel (New York: W. W. Norton, 2018).

[6b] C. Mucci, "Psychoanalysis for a New Humanism: Embodied Testimony, Connectedness, Memory and Forgiveness for a 'Persistence of the Human,'" *International Forum of Psychoanalysis* 27, no. 3 (2018): 176–187. doi:10.1080/0803706X.2017.1362502.

[6c] F. W. Putnam, *Dissociation in Children and Adolescents: A Developmental Perspective* (New York: Guilford Press, 1997).

[6d] A. N. Schore, "Early Organization of the Nonlinear Right Brain and Development of a Predisposition to Psychiatric Disorders," *Development and Psychopathology* 9, no. 4 (1997): 595–631. doi:10.1017/S0954579497001363.

[6e] B. A. van der Kolk, O. van der Hart, and C. R. Marmar, "Dissociation and Information Processing in Posttraumatic Stress Disorder," in *Traumatic Stress: The Effects of Overwhelming Experience on Mind, Body, and Society*, ed. B. A. van der Kolk, A. C. McFarlane, and L. Weisaeth (New York: Guilford Press, 1996), 303–327.

Chapter 5— Stigmatized: The Shame Behind the Mental Health Discussion
[1] The White House Office of the First Lady, Remarks by the First Lady at "Change Direction" Mental Health Event (2015), accessed April 15, 2023, at https://obamawhitehouse.archives.gov/the-press-office/2015/03/04/remarks-first-lady-change-direction-mental-health-event.

[2] B. G. Link and J. C. Phelan, "Conceptualising Stigma," *Annual Review of Sociology* 27, no. 1 (2001): 363–385. doi:10.1146/annurev.soc.27.1.363.

[3] S. Rosenfield, "Labeling Mental Illness: The Effects of Received Services and Perceived Stigma on Life Satisfaction," *American Journal of Sociology* 62, no. 4 (1997): 660–672. doi:10.2307/2657432.

[4a] L. R. Snowden, "African American Service Use for Mental Health Problems," *Journal of Community Psychology* 27 (1999): 303–319. doi:10.1002/(SICI)1520-6629(199905)27:3<303::AIDJCOP5>3.0.CO;2-9.

[4b] K. Wells, R. Klap, A. Koike, and C. Sherbourne, "Ethnic Disparities in Unmet Need for Alcoholism, Drug Abuse, and Mental Health Care," *American Journal of Psychiatry* 158 (2001): 2027–2032. doi:10.1176/appi.ajp.158.12.2027.

[4c] V. D. Ojeda and T. G. McGuire, "Gender and Racial/Ethnic Differences in Use of Outpatient Mental Health and Substance Use Services by Depressed Adults," *Psychiatric Quarterly* 77 (2006): 211–222. doi:10.1007/s11126-006-9008-9.

[5] W. P. Hornung, A. Kieserg, R. Feldmann, and G. Buchkremer, "Psychoeducational Training for Schizophrenic Patients: Background, Procedure and Empirical Findings," *Patient Education and Counseling* 29 (1996): 257–268. doi:10.1016/S0738-3991(96)00918-4.

[6] P. Borges [CRAZYWISE Conversations], *Gabor Maté: Authenticity vs. Attachment* [Video] (YouTube, May 14, 2019). www.youtube.com/watch?v=l3bynimi8HQ.

Chapter 6—EMDR Therapy: A Deep Exhale

[1] B. A. van der Kolk, *The Body Keeps the Score: Brain, Mind, and Body in the Healing of Trauma* (New York: Penguin, 2015).

[2] EMDR International Association, "About EMDR Therapy: EMDR International Association" (February 10, 2023), accessed March 22, 2023, at www.emdria.org/about-emdr-therapy.

[3] L. Maxfield, "A Clinician's Guide to the Efficacy of EMDR Therapy," *Journal of EMDR Practice and Research [Editorial]* 13, no. 4 (2019): 239–246. doi:10.1891/1933-3196.13.4.239.

[4] B. A. van der Kolk, J. Spinazzola, M. E. Blaustein, J. W. Hopper, E. K. Hopper, D. L. Korn, and W. B. Simpson, "A Randomized Clinical Trial of Eye Movement Desensitization and Reprocessing (EMDR), Fluoxetine, and Pill Placebo in the Treatment of Posttraumatic Stress Disorder: Treatment Effects and Long-Term Maintenance," *Journal of Clinical Psychiatry* 68, no. 1 (2007): 37–46. doi:10.4088/jcp.v68n0105.

[5] F. Shapiro and M. S. Forrest, *EMDR: The Breakthrough Therapy for Overcoming Anxiety, Stress, and Trauma* (London: Basic Books, 2016).

[6] F. Shapiro and D. Laliotis, "EMDR and the Adaptive Information Processing Model: Integrative Treatment and Case Conceptualization," *Clinical Social Work Journal* 39, no. 2 (2011): 191–200. doi:10.1007/s10615-010-0300-7.

[7] F. Shapiro, "Eye Movement Desensitization: A New Treatment for Post-Traumatic Stress Disorder," *Journal of Behavior Therapy and Experimental Psychiatry* 20, no. 3 (1989): 211–217. doi:10.1016/0005-7916(89)90025-6.

[8] M. Hase, "The Structure of EMDR Therapy: A Guide for the Therapist," *Frontiers in Psychology* 12 (2021): 660–753. doi:10.3389/fpsyg.2021.660753.

[9] F. Shapiro, *Eye Movement Desensitization and Reprocessing (EMDR): Basic Principles, Protocols, and Procedures* (New York: Guilford Press, 2001).

[10] M. Hase, S. Schallmayer, and M. Sack, "EMDR Reprocessing of the Addiction Memory: Pretreatment, Posttreatment, and 1-Month Follow-Up," *Journal of EMDR Practice and Research* 2, no. 3 (2008): 170–179. doi:10.1891/1933-3196.2.3.170.

Chapter 7— Trauma and Culture

[1a] U. P. Gielen, J. M. Fish, and J. G. Draguns, *Handbook of Culture, Therapy, and Healing* (New Jersey: Lawrence Erlbaum Associates, 2004).

[1b] L. T. Hoshmand, *Culture, Psychotherapy, and Counseling: Critical and Integrative Perspectives* (Thousand Oaks, CA: Sage, 2006).

[2a] A. R. Fischer, L. M. Jone, and D. R. Atkinson, "Reconceptualizing Multicultural Counseling: Universal Healing Conditions in a Culturally Specific Context," *The Counseling Psychologist* 26 (1998): 525–588. doi:10.1177/0011000098264001.

[2b] P. B. Pedersen, "Culturally Biased Assumptions in Counseling Psychology," *The Counseling Psychologist* 31 (2003): 396–403. doi:10.1177/0011000003031004002.

[3a] M. E. Gilfus, "The Price of the Ticket: A Survivor-Centered Appraisal of Trauma Theory," *Violence Against Women* 5 (1999): 1238–1257. doi:10.1177/10778019922183354.

[3b] A. J. Marsella, M. J. Friedman, E. T. Gerrity, and R. M. Scurfield, *Ethnocultural Aspects of Posttraumatic Stress Disorder* (Washington, DC: American Psychological Association, 1996).

[4] B. A. van der Kolk, A. C. McFarlane, and L. Weisaeth, *Traumatic Stress: The Effects of Overwhelming Experience on Mind, Body and Society* (New York: Guilford, 1996).

[5] R. Janoff-Bulman, *Shattered Assumptions: Towards a New Psychology of Trauma* (New York: Free Press, 1992).

6a A. J. Marsella, M. J. Friedman, E. T. Gerrity, and R. M. Scurfield, *Ethnocultural Aspects of Posttraumatic Stress Disorder* (Washington, DC: American Psychological Association, 1996).

6b World Health Organization, *World Report on Violence and Health* (Geneva: World Health Organization, 2002).

7 R. A. Neimeyer, *Lessons of Loss: A Guide to Coping* (New York: McGraw-Hill, 1998).

8 R. Daya, "Buddhist Moments in Psychotherapy," in *Integrating Traditional Healing Practices into Counseling and Psychotherapy*, ed. R. Moodley and W. West (Thousand Oaks, CA: Sage, 2005), 182–193.

9a U. P. Gielen, J. M. Fish, and J. G. Draguns, *Handbook of Culture, Therapy, and Healing* (New Jersey: Lawrence Erlbaum Associates, 2004).

9b R. Moodley and W. West, *Integrating Traditional Healing Practices into Counseling and Psychotherapy* (Thousand Oaks, CA: Sage, 2005).

10 S. Fragoso, *Talk Easy* [Audio Podcast] (November 2020), https://talkeasypod.com/resmaa-menakem.

Chapter 8— Fractured Connections: The Negative Effects of Trauma on Relationships

1 S. M. Johnson, *Hold Me Tight: Seven Conversations for a Lifetime of Love* (New York: Little Brown, 2008).

2 B. A. van der Kolk, "The Neurobiology of Childhood Trauma and Abuse," *Child and Adolescent Psychiatric Clinics of North America* 12, no. 2 (2003): 293–317. doi:10.1016/S1056-4993(03)00003-8.

3 J. Lebow and K. N. Rekart, "Research Assessing Couple and Family Therapies for Posttraumatic Stress Disorder," in *Handbook of Stress, Trauma and the Family*, ed. D. R. Catherall (Abingdon, UK: Routledge, 2013), 261–279.

4a P. K. Kerig and J. F. Alexander, "Family Matters: Integrating Trauma Treatment into Functional Family Therapy for Traumatized Delinquent Youth," *Journal of Child and Adolescent Trauma* 5, no. 3 (2012): 205–223. doi:10.1080/19361521.2012.697103.

4b A. Matsakis, "Trauma and Its Impact on Families," in *Handbook of Stress, Trauma and the Family*, ed. D. R. Catherall (Abingdon, UK: Routledge, 2013), 15–32.

5 J. L. Herman, *Trauma and Recovery: The Aftermath of Violence—from Domestic Abuse to Political Terror* (New York: Basic Books, 1997).

[6] C. R. Figley and K. R. Figley, "Stemming the Tide of Trauma Systemically: The Role of Family Therapy," *Australian and New Zealand Journal of Family Therapy* 30, no. 3 (2009): 173–183. doi:10.1375/ANFT.30.3.173.

[7] S. Guay, V. Billette, and A. Marchand, "Exploring the Links between Post-Traumatic Stress Disorder and Social Support: Processes and Potential Research Avenues," *Journal of Traumatic Stress* 19, no. 3 (2006): 327–338. doi:10.1002/jts.20124.

[8] S. M. Johnson, *Emotionally Focused Couple Therapy with Trauma Survivors: Strengthening Attachment Bonds* (New York: Guilford Press, 2002).

[9] B. A. van der Kolk, "Posttraumatic Stress Disorder and the Nature of Trauma," *Dialogues in Clinical Neuroscience* 2, no. 1 (2000): 7–22. doi:10.31887/DCNS.2000.2.1/bvdkolk.

[10] D. W. Foy, C. B. Eriksson, and G. A. Trice, "Introduction to Group Interventions for Trauma Survivors," *Group Dynamics: Theory, Research, and Practice* 5, no. 4 (2001): 246–251. doi:10.1037/1089-2699.5.4.246.

Chapter 9— The Healing Journey: What Healing Looks Like for Trauma Survivors

[1] B. R. Wainrib, *Healing Crisis and Trauma with Mind, Body, and Spirit* (New York: Springer, 2006).

[2] L. G. Cohen, P. Celnik, A. Pascual-Leone, B. Corwell, L. Falz, J. Dambrosia, et al. "Functional Relevance of Cross-Modal Plasticity in Blind Humans," *Nature* 389 (1997): 180–183. doi:10.1038/38278.

Chapter 10—Broken Children: Helping to Heal the Traumatized Kid in Every Trauma Survivor

[1] K. Cherry, "The Different Types of Attachment Styles," *Verywell Mind* (2022), accessed April 8, 2023, www.verywellmind.com/attachment-styles-2795344.

[2] É. Leblanc, F. Dégeilh, V. Daneault, M. H. Beauchamp, and A. Bernier, "Attachment Security in Infancy: A Preliminary Study of Prospective Links to Brain Morphometry in Late Childhood," *Frontiers in Psychology* 8 (2017): 21–41. doi:10.3389/fpsyg.2017.02141.

[3] J. Cassidy and L. J. Berlin, "The Insecure/Ambivalent Pattern of Attachment: Theory and Research," *Child Development* 65, no. 4 (1994): 971–991. PMID: 7956474.

[4] J. A. Simpson and W. S. Rholes, "Adult Attachment, Stress, and Romantic Relationships," *Current Opinion in Psychology* 13 (2017): 19–24. doi:10.1016/j.copsyc.2016.04.006.